4/17: OX

1

OCT 0 4 2016

Free *From Stress to Success* DVD from Trivium Test Prep

Dear Customer,

Thank you for purchasing from Trivium Test Prep! Whether you're looking to join the military, get into college, or advance your career, we're honored to be a part of your journey.

To show our appreciation (and to help you relieve a little of that test-prep stress), we're offering a **FREE *From Stress to Success* DVD** by Trivium Test Prep. Our DVD includes 35 test preparation strategies that will help keep you calm and collected before and during your big exam. All we ask is that you email us your feedback and describe your experience with our product. Amazing, awful, or just so-so: we want to hear what you have to say!

To receive your **FREE *From Stress to Success* DVD**, please email us at 5star@triviumtestprep.com. Include "Free 5 Star" in the subject line and the following information in your email:

1.   The title of the product you purchased.
2.   Your rating from 1 – 5 (with 5 being the best).
3.   Your feedback about the product, including how our materials helped you meet your goals and ways in which we can improve our products.
4.   Your full name and shipping address so we can send your **FREE *From Stress to Success* DVD**.

If you have any questions or concerns please feel free to contact me directly.

Thank you, and good luck with your studies!

Alyssa Wagoner
Quality Control
alyssa.wagoner@triviumtestprep.com

Table of Contents

Introduction..6

Chapter 1: Reading Placement..8

  Test Your Knowledge: Reading Placement 20

    Test Your Knowledge: Reading Placement – Answers 33

Chapter 2: Writing Skills..34

  Test Your Knowledge: Writing Skills Placement........................ 39

    Test Your Knowledge: Writing Skills Placement – Answers 49

Chapter 3: Writing Essay..50

  Test Your Knowledge: Writing Essay 54

    Test Your Knowledge: Essay – Answers 55

Chapter 4: Math Placement..63

  Test Your Knowledge: Math Achievement and Quantitative Reasoning Question Bank 79

  Test Your Knowledge: Percent/Part/Whole, Percent Change......................... 80

  Test Your Knowledge: Mean, Median, Mode................................... 83

  Test Your Knowledge: Exponents and Roots 86

  Test Your Knowledge: Algebraic Equations.................................... 88

  Test Your Knowledge: Inequalities, Literal Equations, Polynomials, and Binomials.......... 94

  Test Your Knowledge: Slope and Distance to Midpoint............................ 98

  Test Your Knowledge: Absolute Value Equations 105

  Test Your Knowledge: Geometry 110

  Test Your Knowledge: Fundamental Counting Principle, Permutations, Combinations........ 113

  Test Your Knowledge: Ratios, Proportions, Rate of Change........................ 116

Final Thoughts 120

Introduction

Congratulations! If you are reading this book, then it means that you are preparing for the COMPASS, which means you are preparing to further your education. The COMPASS is a great starting point to determine your strengths and weaknesses in areas of math, reading, and writing. This will be used by you and your advisors to plan your coursework, so you get the most out of your education.

About the COMPASS

The COMPASS is a computer-adaptive test, meaning questions will increase or decrease in difficulty depending on if you answer correctly or not. There's no time limit, so you can take as long as you need; although working at a reasonable pace is advised so you don't get mentally fatigued.

Sections on the COMPASS:

- **Reading Placement**: Evaluates skills in reading comprehension, vocabulary, and grammar usage.

- **Writing Skills Placement**: Evaluates skills in punctuation, spelling, capitalization, usage, verb formation/agreement, relationship of clauses, shifts in construction, and organization.

- **Writing Essay Test**: Students will write an essay in response to a single prompt, which will present an issue with two points of view. Students will respond with their own position on the issue.

- **Math Placement**: Evaluates mathematical skills in pre-algebra, algebra, college algebra, geometry, and trigonometry.

- **ESL Tests**: These tests are optional for those who have learned English as a second language. You will be tested on grammar, essay-writing, and reading comprehension. Sound familiar? There are corresponding sections – Reading, Writing, Essay –in the COMPASS exam which cover the exact same materials. Even better: The ESL tests will test these subjects at a low level, so if you become confident with the materials in this study guide, then you will be more than prepared!

How This Book Works

The subsequent chapters in this book are divided into a review of those topics covered on the exam. This is not intended to "teach" or "re-teach" you these concepts – there is no way to cram all of that material into one book! Instead, we are going to help you recall all of the information which you've already learned. Even more importantly, we'll show you how to apply that knowledge.

Each chapter includes an extensive review, with practice drills at the end to test your knowledge. Remember, the COMPASS is not for a grade, but you want to do your best so your time in college is most effective and you don't end up taking classes that don't truly benefit you. With time, practice, and determination, you'll be well-prepared for test day.

Chapter 1: Reading Placement

The COMPASS Reading Placement section consists of several multiple-choice questions, which will measure your ability to understand, analyze, and evaluate written passages. The passages will contain material from a variety of sources, and will cover a number of different topics.

All passages in each section have numbers along the left side of the text which indicate the line number. Questions for each passage will call for knowledge of the following:

1. Specific details and facts.
2. Comparisons and analogies.
3. Inferences.
4. Word meaning through context.
5. Main idea of sections or the passage as a whole.
6. Author's tone and/or point of view.

There are four types of passages which you will encounter: humanities, social studies, natural science, and prose.

The Humanities passage topics are culturally based, focusing on the arts and literature, and can be written journalistically, analytically, or as a personal essay. These tend to portray varying degrees of bias, which you will need to take into account when reading.

The Social Studies passage topics are focused on the workings of civilizations and societies and usually have a political perspective. Take notice of dates, names, chronological order, key concepts, and cause and effect relationships. The authors tend to express controversial views about the subject. It is important that you are able to separate the author's point of view from the general argument.

The Natural Science passages present experiments and scientific theories, along with their implications and reasoning. These are going to include considerable facts and data. Pay attention to comparisons, as well as cause and effect.

The Prose fiction passages are usually excerpts from short stories or novels. You'll want to take note of the plot, characters, style, and tone.

At the end of this chapter, we will have a "Test Your Knowledge" section, which will give you an opportunity to practice reading a passage and answering questions – just as you will on the COMPASS. While a good vocabulary can help, the only way to get better at the reading section is to practice, practice, practice. It is, however, vitally important that you practice the way you want to perform on test day. Form good habits now by actively reading and making notes.

But first, let's freshen up on our reading comprehension skills.

The Main Idea
The main idea of a text is the purpose behind why a writer would choose to write a book, article, story, etc. Being able to find and understand the main idea is a critical skill necessary to comprehend and appreciate what you're reading.

Consider a political election. A candidate is running for office and plans to deliver a speech asserting her position on tax reform. The **topic** of the speech—tax reform—is clear to voters, and probably of interest to many. However, imagine that the candidate believes that taxes should be lowered. She is likely to assert this argument in her speech, supporting it with examples proving why lowering taxes would benefit the public and how it could be accomplished. While the topic of the speech would be tax reform, the benefit of lowering taxes would be the **main idea**. Other candidates may have different perspectives on the topic; they may believe that higher taxes are necessary, or that current taxes are adequate. It is likely that their speeches, while on the same topic of tax reform, would have different main ideas: different arguments likewise supported by different examples. Determining what a speaker, writer, or text is asserting about a specific issue will reveal the main idea.

One more quick note: the exam may also ask about a passage's **theme**, which is similar to but distinct from its topic. While a topic is usually a specific *person, place, thing,* or *issue,* the theme is an *idea* or *concept* that the author refers back to frequently. Examples of common themes include ideas like the importance of family, the dangers of technology, and the beauty of nature.

There will be many questions on the exam that require you to differentiate between the topic, theme, and main idea of a passage. Let's look at an example passage to see how you would answer these questions.

"Babe Didrikson Zaharias, one of the most decorated female athletes of the twentieth century, is an inspiration for everyone. Born in 1911 in Beaumont, Texas, Zaharias lived in a time when women were considered second-class to men, but she never let that stop her from becoming a champion. Babe was one of seven children in a poor immigrant family, and was competitive from an early age. As a child she excelled at most things she tried, especially sports, which continued into high school and beyond. After high school, Babe played amateur basketball for two years, and soon after began training in track and field. Despite the fact that women were only allowed to enter in three events, Babe represented the United States in the 1932 Los Angeles Olympics, and won two gold medals and one silver for track and field events.

"In the early 1930s, Babe began playing golf which earned her a legacy. The first tournament she entered was a men's only tournament, however she did not make the cut to play. Playing golf as an amateur was the only option for a woman at this time, since there was no professional women's league. Babe played as an amateur for a little over a decade, until she turned pro in 1947 for the Ladies Professional Golf Association (LPGA) of which she was a founding member. During her career as a golfer, Babe won eighty-two tournaments, amateur and professional, including the U.S. Women's Open, All-American Open, and British Women's Open Golf Tournament. In 1953, Babe was diagnosed with cancer, but fourteen weeks later, she played in a tournament. That year she won her third U.S. Women's Open. However by 1955, she didn't have the physicality to compete anymore, and she died of the disease in 1956."

The topic of this paragraph is obviously Babe Zaharias—the whole passage describes events from her life. Determining the main idea, however, requires a little more analysis. The passage describes Babe Zaharias' life, but the main idea of the paragraph is what it says *about* her life. To figure out the main idea, consider what the writer is saying about Babe Zaharias. The writer is saying that she's someone to admire—that's the main idea and what unites all the information in the paragraph. Lastly, what might the theme of the passage be? The writer refers to several broad concepts, including never giving up and overcoming the odds, both of which could be themes for the passage. Two major indicators of the main idea of a paragraph or passage follow below:

- It is a general idea; it applies to all the more specific ideas in the passage. Every other sentence in a paragraph should be able to relate in some way to the main idea.

- It asserts a specific viewpoint that the author supports with facts, opinions, or other details. In other words, the main idea takes a stand.

Example

From so far away it's easy to imagine the surface of our solar system's planets as enigmas—how could we ever know what those far-flung planets really look like? It turns out, however, that scientists have a number of tools at their disposal that allow them to paint detailed pictures of many planets' surfaces. The topography of Venus, for example, has been explored by several space probes, including the Russian Venera landers and NASA's Magellan orbiter. These craft used imaging and radar to map the surface of the planet, identifying a whole host of features including volcanoes, craters, and a complex system of channels. Mars has similarly been mapped by space probes, including the famous Mars Rovers, which are automated vehicles that actually landed on the surface of Mars. These rovers have been used by NASA and other space agencies to study the geology, climate, and possible biology of the planet.

In addition these long-range probes, NASA has also used its series of orbiting telescopes to study distant planets. These four massively powerful telescopes include the famous Hubble Space Telescope as well as the Compton Gamma Ray Observatory, Chandra X-Ray Observatory, and the Spitzer Space Telescope. Scientists can use these telescopes to examine planets using not only visible light but also infrared and near-infrared light, ultraviolet light, x-rays and gamma rays.

Powerful telescopes aren't just found in space: NASA makes use of Earth-bound telescopes as well. Scientists at the National Radio Astronomy Observatory in Charlottesville, VA, have spent decades using radio imaging to build an incredibly detailed portrait of Venus' surface. In fact, Earth-bound telescopes offer a distinct advantage over orbiting telescopes because they allow scientists to capture data from a fixed point, which in turn allows them to effectively compare data collected over long period of time.

Which of the following sentences best describes the main of the passage?

A)   It's impossible to know what the surfaces of other planets are really like.
B)   Telescopes are an important tool for scientists studying planets in our solar system.
C)   Venus' surface has many of the same features as the Earth's, including volcanoes, craters, and channels.
D)   Scientists use a variety of advanced technologies to study the surface of the planets in our solar system.

Answer: Answer A) can be eliminated because it directly contradicts the rest of the passage, which goes into detail about how scientists have learned about the surfaces of other planets. Answers B) and C) can also be eliminated because they offer only specific details from the passage—while both choices contain details from the passage, neither is general enough to encompass the passage as a whole. Only answer D) provides an assertion that is both backed up by the passage's content and general enough to cover the entire passage.

Topic and Summary Sentences

The main idea of a paragraph usually appears within the topic sentence. The **topic sentence** introduces the main idea to readers; it indicates not only the topic of a passage, but also the writer's perspective on the topic. Notice, for example, how the first sentence in the example paragraph about Babe Zaharias states the main idea: *Babe Didrikson Zaharias, one of the most decorated female athletes of the twentieth century, is an inspiration for everyone.*

Even though paragraphs generally begin with topic sentences due to their introductory nature, on occasion writers build up to the topic sentence by using supporting details in order to generate interest or build an argument. Be alert for paragraphs when writers do not include a clear topic sentence at all; even without a clear topic sentence, a paragraph will still have a main idea. You may also see a **summary sentence** at the end of a passage. As its name suggests, this sentence sums up the passage, often by restating the main idea and the author's key evidence supporting it.

Example

In the following paragraph, what are the topic and summary sentences?

The Constitution of the United States establishes a series of limits to rein in centralized power. Separation of powers distributes federal authority among three competing branches: the executive, the legislative, and the judicial. Checks and balances allow the branches to check the usurpation of power by any one branch. States' rights are protected under the Constitution from too much encroachment by the federal government. Enumeration of powers names the specific and few powers the federal government has. These four restrictions have helped sustain the American republic for over two centuries.

Answer: The topic sentence is the first sentence in the paragraph. It introduces the topic of discussion, in this case the constitutional limits aimed at resisting centralized power. The summary sentence is the last sentence in the paragraph. It sums up the information that was just presented: here, that constitutional limits have helped sustain the United States of America for over two hundred years.

Implied Main Idea

A paragraph without a clear topic sentence still has a main idea; rather than clearly stated, it is implied. Determining the **implied main idea** requires some detective work: you will need to look at the author's word choice and tone in addition to the content of the passage to find his or her main idea. Let's look at an example paragraph.

Example

One of my summer reading books was Mockingjay. *Though it's several hundred pages long, I read it in just a few days. I was captivated by the adventures of the main character and the complicated plot of the book. However, I felt like the ending didn't reflect the excitement of the story. Given what a powerful personality the main character has, I felt like the ending didn't do her justice.*

> Even without a clear topic sentence, this paragraph has a main idea. What is the writer's perspective on the book—what is the writer saying about it?
>
> A) *Mockingjay* is a terrific novel.
> B) *Mockingjay* is disappointing.
> C) *Mockingjay* is full of suspense.
> D) *Mockingjay* is a lousy novel.

The correct answer is B): the novel is disappointing. The process of elimination will reveal the correct answer if that is not immediately clear. While that the paragraph begins with positive commentary on the book—*I was captivated by the adventures of the main character and the complicated plot of the book*—this positive idea is followed by the contradictory transition word *however.* A) cannot be the correct answer because the author concludes that the novel was poor. Likewise, D) cannot be correct because it does not encompass all the ideas in the paragraph; despite the negative conclusion, the author enjoyed most of the book. The main idea should be able to encompass all of the thoughts in a paragraph; choice D) does not apply to the beginning of this paragraph. Finally, choice C) is too specific; it could only apply to the brief description of the plot and adventures of the main character. That leaves choice B) as the best option. The author initially enjoyed the book, but was disappointed by the ending, which seemed unworthy of the exciting plot and character.

Fortunately, none of Alyssa's coworkers has ever seen inside the large filing drawer in her desk. Disguised by the meticulous neatness of the rest of her workspace, there was no sign of the chaos beneath. To even open it, she had to struggle for several minutes with the enormous pile of junk jamming the drawer, until it would suddenly give way, and papers, folders, and candy wrappers spilled out of the top and onto the floor. It was an organizational nightmare, with torn notes and spreadsheets haphazardly thrown on top of each other, and melted candy smeared across pages. She was worried the odor would soon permeate to her coworker's desks, revealing to them her secret.

Which sentence best describes the main idea of the paragraph above?

A) Alyssa wishes she could move to a new desk.
B) Alyssa wishes she had her own office.
C) Alyssa is glad none of her coworkers know about her messy drawer.
D) Alyssa is sad because she doesn't have any coworkers.

Clearly, Alyssa has a messy drawer, and C) is the right answer. The paragraph begins by indicating her gratitude that her coworkers do not know about her drawer (*Fortunately, none of Alyssa's coworkers has ever seen inside the large filing drawer in her desk.*) Plus, notice how the drawer is described: *it was an organizational nightmare*, and it apparently doesn't even function properly: *to even open the drawer, she had to struggle for several minutes.* The writer reveals that it has an odor, with *melted candy* inside. Alyssa is clearly ashamed of her drawer and fearful of being judged by her coworkers for it.

Specific Details and Facts
Specific details and facts provide more support for the author's main idea. For instance, in the Babe Zaharias example above, the writer makes the general assertion that *Babe Didrikson Zaharias, one of the most decorated female athletes of the twentieth century, is an inspiration for everyone.* The other sentences offer specific facts and details that prove why Babe Zaharias is an inspiration: the struggles she faced as a female athlete, and the specific years she competed in the Olympics and in golf.

Writers often provide clues that can help you identify supporting details. These **signal words** tell you that a supporting fact or idea will follow, and so can be helpful in identifying supporting details. Signal words can also help you rule out sentences that are not the main idea or topic sentence: if a sentence begins with one of these phrases, it will likely be too specific to be a main idea.

Questions on the COMPASS will ask you to do two things with supporting details: you will need to find details that support a particular idea and also explain why a particular detail was included in the passage. In order to answer these questions, you need to have a solid understanding of the passage's main idea. With this knowledge, you can determine how a supporting detail fits in with the larger structure of the passage.

Example

From so far away it's easy to imagine the surface of our solar system's planets as enigmas—how could we ever know what those far-flung planets really look like? It turns out, however, that scientists have a number of tools at their disposal that allow them to paint detailed pictures of many planets' surfaces. The topography of Venus, for example, has been explored by several space probes, including the Russian *Venera* landers and NASA's *Magellan* orbiter. These craft used imaging and radar to map the surface of the planet, identifying a whole host of features including volcanoes, craters, and a complex system of channels. Mars has similarly been mapped by space probes, including the famous Mars Rovers, which are automated vehicles that actually landed on the surface of Mars. These rovers have been used by NASA and other space agencies to study the geology, climate, and possible biology of the planet.

In addition these long-range probes, NASA has also used its series of orbiting telescopes to study distant planets. These four massively powerful telescopes include the famous Hubble Space Telescope as well as the Compton Gamma Ray Observatory, Chandra X-Ray Observatory, and the Spitzer Space Telescope. Scientists can use these telescopes to examine planets using not only visible light but also infrared and near-infrared light, ultraviolet light, x-rays and gamma rays.

Powerful telescopes aren't just found in space: NASA makes use of Earth-bound telescopes as well. Scientists at the National Radio Astronomy Observatory in Charlottesville, VA, have spent decades using radio imaging to build an incredibly detailed portrait of Venus' surface. In fact, Earth-bound telescopes offer a distinct advantage over orbiting telescopes because they allow scientists to capture data from a fixed point, which in turn allows them to effectively compare data collected over long period of time.

Which sentence from the text best helps develop the idea that scientists make use of many different technologies to study the surfaces of other planets?

A)   These rovers have been used by NASA and other space agencies to study the geology, climate, and possible biology of the planet.
B)   From so far away it's easy to imagine the surface of our solar system's planets as enigmas—how could we ever know what those far-flung planets really look like?
C)   In addition these long-range probes, NASA has also used its series of orbiting telescopes to study distant planets.
D)   These craft used imaging and radar to map the surface of the planet, identifying a whole host of features including volcanoes, craters, and a complex system of channels.

Answer: You're looking for detail from the passage that supports the main idea—scientists make use of many different technologies to study the surfaces of other planets. Answer A) includes a specific detail about rovers, but does not offer any details that support the idea of multiple technologies being used. Similarly, answer D) provides another specific detail about space probes. Answer B) doesn't provide any supporting details; it simply introduces the topic of the passage. Only answer C) provides a detail that directly supports the author's assertion that scientists use multiple technologies to study the planets.

If true, which detail could be added to the passage above to support the author's argument that scientists use many different technologies to study the surface of planets?

A)   Because the Earth's atmosphere blocks x-rays, gamma rays, and infrared radiation, NASA needed to put telescopes in orbit above the atmosphere.

B)   In 2015, NASA released a map of Venus which was created by compiling images from orbiting telescopes and long-range space probes.

C)   NASA is currently using the *Curiosity* and *Opportunity* rovers to look for signs of ancient life on Mars.

D)   NASA has spent over $2.5 billion to build, launch, and repair the Hubble Space Telescope.

Answer: You can eliminate answers C) and D) because they don't address the topic of studying the surface of planets. Answer A) can also be eliminated because it only addresses a single technology. Only choice B) provides would add support to the author's claim about the importance of using multiple technologies.

The author likely included the detail *Earth-bound telescopes offer a distinct advantage over orbiting telescopes because they allow scientists to capture data from a fixed point* in order to:

A)   Explain why it has taken scientists so long to map the surface of Venus.

B)   Suggest that Earth-bound telescopes are the most important equipment used by NASA scientists.

C)   Prove that orbiting telescopes will soon be replaced by Earth-bound telescopes.

D)   Demonstrate why NASA scientists rely on my different types of scientific equipment.

Answer: Only answer D) directs directly to the author's main argument. The author doesn't mention how long it has taken to map the surface of Venus (answer A), nor does he say that one technology is more important than the others (answer B). And while this detail does highlight the advantages of using Earth-bound telescopes, the author's argument is that many technologies are being used at the same time, so there's no reason to think that orbiting telescopes will be replaced (answer C).

Facts vs. Opinions
On the exam Reading passages you might be asked to identify a statement in a passage as either a fact or an opinion, so you'll need to know the difference between the two. A **fact** is a statement or thought that can be proven to be true. The statement *Wednesday comes after Tuesday* is a fact—you can point to a calendar to prove it. In contrast, an **opinion** is an assumption that is not based in fact and cannot be proven to be true. The assertion that *television is more entertaining than feature films* is an opinion—people will disagree on this, and there's no reference you can use to prove or disprove it.

Example
Exercise is critical for healthy development in children. Today, there is an epidemic of unhealthy children in the United States who will face health problems in adulthood due to poor diet and lack of exercise as children. This is a problem for all Americans, especially with the rising cost of healthcare.
It is vital that school systems and parents encourage their children to engage in a minimum of thirty minutes of cardiovascular exercise each day, mildly increasing their heart rate for a sustained period. This is proven to decrease the likelihood of developmental diabetes, obesity, and a multitude of other health problems. Also, children need a proper diet rich in fruits and vegetables so that they can grow and develop physically, as well as learn healthy eating habits early on.
                Which of the following is a fact in the passage, not an opinion?

A) Fruits and vegetables are the best way to help children be healthy.
B) Children today are lazier than they were in previous generations.
C) The risk of diabetes in children is reduced by physical activity.
D) Children should engage in thirty minutes of exercise a day.

Answer: Choice B) can be discarded immediately because it is negative and is not discussed anywhere in the passage. Answers A) and D) are both opinions—the author is promoting exercise, fruits, and vegetables as a way to make children healthy. (Notice that these incorrect answers contain words that hint at being an opinion such as *best*, *should*, or other comparisons.) Answer B), on the other hand, is a simple fact stated by the author; it's introduced by the word *proven* to indicate that you don't need to just take the author's word for it.

The Author's Purpose and Tone

Whenever an author writes a text, she always has a purpose, whether that's to entertain, inform, explain, or persuade. A short story, for example, is meant to entertain, while an online news article would be designed to inform the public about a current event.

Each of these different types of writing has a specific name. On the exam, you may be asked to identify which of these categories a passage fits into:

- **Narrative writing** tells a story. (novel, short story, play)
- **Expository writing** informs people. (newspaper and magazine articles)
- **Technical writing** explains something. (product manual, directions)
- **Persuasive writing** tries to convince the reader of something. (opinion column on a blog)

You may also be asked about primary and secondary sources. These terms describe not the writing itself but the author's relationship to what's being written about. A **primary source** is an unaltered piece of writing that was composed during the time when the events being described took place; these texts are often written by the people involved. A **secondary source** might address the same topic but provides extra commentary or analysis. These texts can be written by people not directly involved in the events. For example, a book written by a political candidate to inform people about his or her stand on an issue is a primary source; an online article written by a journalist analyzing how that position will affect the election is a secondary source.

Example

Elizabeth closed her eyes and braced herself on the armrests that divided her from her fellow passengers. Take-off was always the worst part for her. The revving of the engines, the way her stomach dropped as the plane lurched upward: it made her feel sick. Then, she had to watch the world fade away beneath her, getting smaller and smaller until it was just her and the clouds hurtling through the sky. Sometimes (but only sometimes) it just had to be endured, though. She focused on the thought of her sister's smiling face and her new baby nephew as the plane slowly pulled onto the runway.

The passage above is reflective of which type of writing?
A) Narrative
B) Expository
C) Technical
D) Persuasive

Answer: The passage is telling a story—we meet Elizabeth and learn about her fear of flying—so it's a narrative text. There is no factual information presented or explained, nor is the author trying to persuade the reader.

Inferences and Drawing Conclusions
In addition to understanding the main idea and factual content of a passage, you'll also be asked to take your analysis one step further and anticipate what other information could logically be added to the passage. In a non-fiction passage, for example, you might be asked which statement the author of the passage would agree with. In an excerpt from a fictional work, you might be asked to anticipate what the character would do next.

To answer these questions, you need to have a solid understanding of the topic, theme, and main idea of the passage; armed with this information, you can figure out which of the answer choices best fits within those criteria (or alternatively, which ones do not). For example, if the author of the passage is advocating for safer working conditions in textile factories, any supporting details that would be added to the passage should support that idea. You might add sentences that contain information about the number of accidents that occur in textile factories or that outline a new plan for fire safety.

Example
Today, there is an epidemic of unhealthy children in the United States who will face health problems in adulthood due to poor diet and lack of exercise during their childhood. This is a problem for all Americans, as adults with chronic health issues are adding to the rising cost of healthcare. A child who grows up living an unhealthy lifestyle is likely to become an adult who does the same.

Because exercise is critical for healthy development in children, it is vital that school systems and parents encourage their children to engage in a minimum of thirty minutes of cardiovascular exercise each day. Even this small amount of exercise has been proven to decrease the likelihood that young people will develop diabetes, obesity, and other health issues as adults. In addition to exercise, children need a proper diet rich in fruits and vegetables so that they can grow and develop physically. Starting a good diet early also teaches children healthy eating habits they will carry into adulthood.

    The author of this passage would most likely agree with which statement?
    A)   Parents are solely responsible for the health of their children.
    B)   Children who do not want to exercise should not be made to.
    C)   Improved childhood nutrition will help lower the amount Americans spend on healthcare.
    D)   It's not important to teach children healthy eating habits because they will learn them as adults.

Answer: The author would most likely support answer C): he mentions in the first paragraph that unhealthy habits are adding to the rising cost of healthcare. The main idea of the passage is that nutrition and exercise are important for children, so answer B) doesn't make sense—the author would likely support measures to encourage children to exercise. Answers A) and D) can also be eliminated because they are directly contradicted in the text. The author specifically mentions the role of schools systems, so he doesn't believe parents are solely responsible for their children's health. He also specifically states that children who grow up with unhealthy habit will become adults with unhealthy habits, which contradicts D).

Elizabeth closed her eyes and braced herself on the armrests that divided her from her fellow passengers. Take-off was always the worst part for her. The revving of the engines, the way her stomach dropped as the plane lurched upward: it made her feel sick. Then, she had to watch the world fade away beneath her, getting smaller and smaller until it was just her and the clouds hurtling through the sky. Sometimes (but only sometimes) it just had to be endured, though. She focused on the thought of her sister's smiling face and her new baby nephew as the plane slowly pulled onto the runway.

Which of the following is Elizabeth least likely to do in the future?
A)   Take a flight to her brother's wedding.
B)   Apply for a job as a flight attendant.
C)   Never board an airplane again.
D)   Get sick on an airplane.

Answer: It's clear from the passage that Elizabeth hates flying, but it willing to endure it for the sake of visiting her family. Thus, it seems likely that she would be willing to get on a plane for her brother's wedding, making A) and C) incorrect answers. The passage also explicitly tells us that she feels sick on planes, so D) is likely to happen. We can infer, though, that she would not enjoy being on an airplane for work, so she's very unlikely to apply for a job as a flight attendant, which is choice B).

Word and Phrase Meaning Through Context
On the Reading section you may also be asked to provide definitions or intended meanings for words within passages. You may have never encountered some of these words before the test, but there are tricks you can use to figure out what they mean.

Context Clues
The most fundamental vocabulary skill is using the context in which a word is used to determine its meaning. Your ability to observe sentences closely is extremely useful when it comes to understanding new vocabulary words.

There are two types of context that can help you understand the meaning of unfamiliar words: situational context and sentence context. Regardless of which context is present, these types of questions are not really testing your knowledge of vocabulary; rather, they test your ability to comprehend the meaning of a word through its usage.

Situational context is context that is presented by the setting or circumstances in which a word or phrase occurs. **Sentence context** occurs within the specific sentence that contains the vocabulary word. To figure out words using sentence context clues, you should first determine the most important words in the sentence.

There are four types of clues that can help you understand context, and therefore the meaning of a word:

- **Restatement** clues occur when the definition of the word is clearly stated in the sentence.
- **Positive/negative clues** can tell you whether a word has a positive or negative meaning.
- **Contrast clues** include the opposite meaning of a word. Words like *but, on the other hand,* and *however* are tip-offs that a sentence contains a contrast clue.
- **Specific detail clues** provide a precise detail that can help you understand the meaning of the word.

It is important to remember that more than one of these clues can be present in the same sentence. The more there are, the easier it will be to determine the meaning of the word. For example, the following sentence uses both restatement and positive/negative clues: *Janet suddenly found herself destitute, so poor she could barely afford to eat.* The second part of the sentence clearly indicates that *destitute* is a negative word. It also restates the meaning: very poor.

Examples

I had a hard time reading her *illegible* handwriting.
A)   neat
B)   unsafe
C)   sloppy
D)   educated

Answer: Already, you know that this sentence is discussing something that is hard to read. Look at the word that *illegible* is describing: handwriting. Based on context clues, you can tell that *illegible* means that her handwriting is hard to read.

Next, look at the answer choices. Choice A), *neat,* is obviously a wrong answer because neat handwriting would not be difficult to read. Choices B) and D), *unsafe* and *educated,* don't make sense. Therefore, choice C), *sloppy,* is the best answer.

The dog was *dauntless* in the face of danger, braving the fire to save the girl trapped inside the building.
A)   difficult
B)   fearless
C)   imaginative
D)   startled

Answer: Demonstrating bravery in the face of danger would be B) *fearless.* In this case, the restatement clue (*braving the fire*) tells you exactly what the word means.

Beth did not spend any time preparing for the test, but Tyrone kept a *rigorous* study schedule.
A)   strict
B)   loose
C)   boring
D)   strange

Answer: In this case, the contrast word *but* tells us that Tyrone studied in a different way than Beth, which means it's a contrast clue. If Beth did not study hard, then Tyrone did. The best answer, therefore, is choice A).

Analyzing Words
As you no doubt know, determining the meaning of a word can be more complicated than just looking in a dictionary. A word might have more than one **denotation**, or definition; which one the author intends can only be judged by looking at the surrounding text. For example, the word *quack* can refer to the sound a duck makes, or to a person who publicly pretends to have a qualification which he or she does not actually possess.

A word may also have different **connotations**, which are the implied meanings and emotion a word evokes in the reader. For example, a cubicle is a simply a walled desk in an office, but for many the word implies a constrictive, uninspiring workplace. Connotations can vary greatly between cultures and even between individuals.

Lastly, authors might make use of **figurative language**, which is the use of a word to imply something other than the word's literal definition. This is often done by comparing two things. If you say *I felt like a butterfly when I got a new haircut*, the listener knows you don't resemble an insect but instead felt beautiful and transformed.

Word Structure

Although you are not expected to know every word in the English language for your test, you will need the ability to use deductive reasoning to find the choice that is the best match for the word in question, which is why we are going to explain how to break a word into its parts to determine its meaning. Many words can be broken down into three main parts:

prefix – root – suffix

Roots are the building blocks of all words. Every word is either a root itself or has a root. Just as a plant cannot grow without roots, neither can vocabulary, because a word must have a root to give it meaning. The root is what is left when you strip away all the prefixes and suffixes from a word. For example, in the word *unclear*, if you take away the prefix *un-*, you have the root *clear*.

Roots are not always recognizable words, because they generally come from Latin or Greek words, such as *nat*, a Latin root meaning born. The word *native*, which means a person born in a referenced placed, comes from this root, so does the word *prenatal*, meaning before birth. It's important to keep in mind, however, that roots do not always match the exact definitions of words, and they can have several different spellings.

Prefixes are syllables added to the beginning of a word and **suffixes** are syllables added to the end of the word. Both carry assigned meanings and can be attached to a word to completely change the word's meaning or to enhance the word's original meaning.

Let's use the word prefix itself as an example: *fix* means to place something securely and *pre-* means before. Therefore, *prefix* means to place something before or in front. Now let's look at a suffix: in the word *feminism*, *femin* is a root which means female. The suffix *-ism* means act, practice, or process. Thus, *feminism* is the process of establishing equal rights for women.

Although you cannot determine the meaning of a word by a prefix or suffix alone, you can use this knowledge to eliminate answer choices; understanding whether the word is positive or negative can give you the partial meaning of the word.

Questions 1 – 4 are based on the following passage:

From *"On Lying Awake at Night"* by Stewart Edward White *(public domain)*:

About once in so often you are due to lie awake at night. Why this is so I have never been able to discover. It apparently comes from no predisposing uneasiness of indigestion, no rashness in the matter of too much tea or tobacco, no excitation of unusual incident or stimulating conversation. In fact, you turn in with the expectation of rather a good night's rest. Almost at once the little noises of the forest grow larger, blend in the hollow bigness of the first drowse; your thoughts drift idly back and forth between reality and dream; when—*snap!*—you are broad awake!

For, unlike mere insomnia, lying awake at night in the woods is pleasant. The eager, nervous straining for sleep gives way to a delicious indifference. You do not care. Your mind is cradled in an exquisite poppy-suspension of judgment and of thought. Impressions slip vaguely into your consciousness and as vaguely out again. Sometimes they stand stark and naked for your inspection; sometimes they lose themselves in the mist of half-sleep. Always they lay soft velvet fingers on the drowsy imagination, so that in their caressing you feel the vaster spaces from which they have come. Peaceful-brooding your *faculties* receive. Hearing, sight, smell—all are preternaturally keen to whatever of sound and sight and woods perfume is abroad through the night; and yet at the same time active appreciation dozes, so these things lie on it sweet and cloying like fallen rose-leaves.

Nothing is more fantastically unreal to tell about, nothing more concretely real to experience, than this undernote of the quick water. And when you do lie awake at night, it is always making its unobtrusive appeal. Gradually its hypnotic spell works. The distant chimes ring louder and nearer as you cross the borderland of sleep. And then outside the tent some little woods noise snaps the thread. An owl hoots, a whippoorwill cries, a twig cracks beneath the cautious prowl of some night creature—at once the yellow sunlit French meadows puff away—you are staring at the blurred image of the moon spraying through the texture of your tent.

(You have cast from you with the warm blanket the drowsiness of dreams. A coolness, physical and spiritual, bathes you from head to foot. All your senses are keyed to the last vibrations. You hear the littler night prowlers; you glimpse the greater. A faint, searching woods perfume of dampness greets your nostrils. And somehow, mysteriously, in a manner not to be understood, the forces of the world seem in suspense, as though a touch might crystallize infinite possibilities into infinite power and motion. But the touch lacks. The forces hover on the edge of action, unheeding the little noises. In all humbleness and awe, you are a dweller of the Silent Places.

The night wind from the river, or from the open spaces of the wilds, chills you after a time. You begin to think of your blankets. In a few moments you roll yourself in their soft wool. Instantly it is morning.

And, strange to say, you have not to pay by going through the day unrefreshed. You may feel like turning in at eight instead of nine, and you may fall asleep with unusual promptitude, but your journey will begin clear-headedly, proceed springily, and end with much in reserve. No languor, no dull headache, no exhaustion, follows your experience. For this once your two hours of sleep have been as effective as nine.

1. In Paragraph 2, "faculties" is used to mean:
    a) Teachers.
    b) Senses.
    c) Imaginations.
    d) Capacities.

2. The author's opinion of insomnia is that:
    a) It is not a problem because nights without sleep are refreshing.
    b) It can happen more often when sleeping in the woods because of the noises in nature.
    c) It is generally unpleasant, but sometimes can be hypnotic.
    d) It is the best way to cultivate imagination.

3. By "strange to say" in Paragraph 6, the author means:
    a) The experience of the night before had an unreal quality.
    b) The language used in describing the night before is not easily understood.
    c) It is not considered acceptable to express the opinion the author expresses.
    d) Contrary to expectations, one is well-rested after the night before.

4. How is this essay best characterized?
    a) A playful examination of a common medical problem.
    b) A curious look at both sides of an issue.
    c) A fanciful description of the author's experience.
    d) A horrific depiction of night hallucinations.

Questions 5-10 are based on the following passages:

Passage One
An excerpt from the essay *"Tradition and the Individual Talent"* by T.S. Eliot (public domain):

No poet, no artist of any art, has his complete meaning alone. His significance, his appreciation is the appreciation of his relation to the dead poets and artists. You cannot value him alone; you must set him, for contrast and comparison, among the dead. I mean this as a principle of aesthetic, not merely historical, criticism. The necessity that he shall conform, that he shall cohere, is not one-sided; what happens when a new work of art is created is something that happens simultaneously to all the works of art which preceded it. The existing monuments form an ideal order among themselves, which is modified by the introduction of the new (the really new) work of art among them. The existing order is complete before the new work arrives; for order to persist after the supervention of novelty, the *whole* existing order must be, if ever so slightly, altered; and so the relations, proportions, values of each work of art toward the whole are readjusted; and this is conformity between the old and the new. Whoever has approved this idea of order, of the form of European, of English literature, will not find it preposterous that the past should be altered by the present as much as the present is directed by the past. And the poet who is aware of this will be aware of great difficulties and responsibilities.

Passage Two
An excerpt from the Clive Bell's seminal art history book "*Art*" (public domain):

To criticize a work of art historically is to play the science-besotted fool. No more disastrous theory ever issued from the brain of a charlatan than that of evolution in art. Giotto[1] did not creep, a grub, that Titian[2] might flaunt, a butterfly. To think of a man's art as leading on to the art of someone else is to misunderstand it. To praise or abuse or be interested in a work of art because it leads or does not lead to another work of art is to treat it as though it were not a work of art. The connection of one work of art with another may have everything to do with history: it has nothing to do with appreciation. So soon as we begin to consider a work as anything else than an end in itself we leave the world of art. Though the development of painting from Giotto to Titian may be interesting historically, it cannot affect the value of any particular picture: aesthetically, it is of no consequence whatever. Every work of art must be judged on its own merits.

5. In Passage One, the word "cohere" is used to most closely mean:
    a) To be congruous with.
    b) To supplant.
    c) To imitate.
    d) To overhaul.
    e) To deviate from.

6. In Passage Two, the author alludes to a butterfly to contradict which concept?
    a) The theory of evolution is responsible for the discipline of art criticism.
    b) Scientific knowledge is not necessary to understand paintings.
    c) Artists who show off are doomed to be criticized.
    d) Art which finds inspiration in nature is the highest form of art.
    e) Titian's art is beautiful as a result of the horrible art that came before.

7. The author of Passage One would be most likely to support:
    a) An artist who imitated the great works of the past.
    b) An art critic who relied solely on evaluating the aesthetics of new art.
    c) A historian who studied the aesthetic evolution of art.
    d) An artist who was also a scientist.
    e) An artist who shouldered the burden of creating something new, while affecting the old, in the world of art.

8. The meaning of the sentence "To praise or abuse or be interested in a work of art because it leads or does not lead to another work of art is to treat it as though it were not a work of art" in Passage 2 means:
    a) Works of art cannot be judged primarily by their relation to one another.
    b) One should not vandalize works of art.
    c) It is necessary to understand how one work of art leads to another in order to judge it.
    d) Works of art must be treated with respect.
    e) Understanding works of art is reliant on seeing them on a historical scale.

9. The author of Passage One would likely agree with which of the following statements?
    a) The past is a monument that is unalterable by the present.

---

[1] Giotto was an Italian painter during the Middle Ages.
[2] Titian was an Italian painter during the Renaissance.

b) Historical knowledge is entirely separate from artistic knowledge.
c) To understand a novel written in the twentieth century, it is necessary to have some knowledge of nineteenth century literature.
d) Painters of Italian descent are all related to one another.
e) One cannot be a scholar of literary history without also being a scholar of scientific thought.

10. The authors of both passages would likely agree with which of the following statements?
   a) An aesthetic judgment is the greatest possible approach to art criticism.
   b) Knowledge of history compromises one's ability to criticize works of art.
   c) The painter Titian was able to create his art as a consequence of the art which came before his time.
   d) It is imperative to understand the progression from one work of art to another.
   e) Not all works of art are consequential.

Questions 11 and 12 are based on the following passage:

Excerpt from Anne Walker's "*A Matter of Proportion*," a short science-fiction story published in 1959 (public domain). In this excerpt, one character tells another about an injured man who is planning a secret operation:

On the way, he filled in background. Scott had been living out of the hospital in a small apartment, enjoying as much liberty as he could manage. He had equipment so he could stump around, and an antique car specially equipped. He wasn't complimentary about them. Orthopedic products had to be: unreliable, hard to service, unsightly, intricate, and uncomfortable. If they also squeaked and cut your clothes, fine!

Having to plan every move with an eye on weather and a dozen other factors, he developed an uncanny foresight. Yet he had to improvise at a moment's notice. With life a continuous high-wire act, he trained every surviving fiber to precision, dexterity, and tenacity. Finally, he avoided help. Not pride, self-preservation; the compulsively helpful have rarely the wit to ask before rushing in to knock you on your face, so he learned to bide his time till the horizon was clear of beaming simpletons. Also, he found an interest in how far he could go.

11. Why does Scott primarily avoid the help of others?
   a) He has found that he is usually better off without it.
   b) He does not want to rely on other people for anything.
   c) He is doing experiments to test his own limits.
   d) He is working on a secret operation and cannot risk discovery.
   e) He does not realize that he needs assistance.

12. "Orthopedic" in paragraph one most nearly means:
   a) Uncomfortable.
   b) Dangerous.
   c) Corrective.
   d) Enhanced.
   e) Complicated.

Excerpt from Rennie W. Doane's *"Insects and Disease,"* a popular science account published in 1910 (public domain):

It has been estimated that there are about four thousand species or kinds of Protozoans, about twenty-five thousand species of Mollusks, about ten thousand species of birds, about three thousand five hundred species of mammals, and from two hundred thousand to one million species of insects, or from two to five times as many kinds of insects as all other animals combined.

Not only do the insects preponderate in number of species, but the number of individuals belonging to many of the species is absolutely beyond our comprehension. Try to count the number of little green aphis on a single infested rose-bush, or on a cabbage plant; guess at the number of mosquitoes issuing each day from a good breeding-pond; estimate the number of scale insects on a single square inch of a tree badly infested with San José scale; then try to think how many more bushes or trees or ponds may be breeding their millions just as these and you will only begin to comprehend the meaning of this statement.

As long as these myriads of insects keep, in what we are pleased to call their proper place, we care not for their numbers and think little of them except as some student points out some wonderful thing about their structure, life-history or adaptations. But since the dawn of history we find accounts to show that insects have not always kept to their proper sphere but have insisted at various times and in various ways in interfering with man's plans and wishes, and on account of their excessive numbers the results have often been most disastrous.

Insects cause an annual loss to the people of the United States of over $1,000,000,000. Grain fields are devastated; orchards and gardens are destroyed or seriously affected; forests are made waste places and in scores of other ways these little pests which do not keep in their proper places are exacting this tremendous tax from our people. These things have been known and recognized for centuries, and scores of volumes have been written about the insects and their ways and of methods of combating them.

Yellow fever, while not so widespread as malaria, is more fatal and therefore more terrorizing. Its presence and spread are due entirely to a single species of mosquito, *Stegomyia calopus*. While this species is usually restricted to tropical or semi-tropical regions it sometimes makes its appearance in places farther north, especially in summer time, where it may thrive for a time. The adult mosquito is black, conspicuously marked with white. The legs and abdomen are banded with white and on the thorax is a series of white lines which in well-preserved specimens distinctly resembles a lyre. These mosquitoes are essentially domestic insects, for they are very rarely found except in houses or in their immediate vicinity. Once they enter a room they will scarcely leave it except to lay their eggs in a near-by cistern, water-pot, or some other convenient place.

Their habit of biting in the daytime has gained for them the name of "day mosquitoes" to distinguish them from the night feeders. But they will bite at night as well as by day and many other species are not at all adverse to a daylight meal, if the opportunity offers, so this habit is not distinctive. The recognition of these facts has a distinct bearing in the methods adopted to prevent the spread of yellow fever. There are no striking characters or habits in the larval or pupal stages that would enable us to distinguish without careful examination this species from other similar forms with which it might be associated. For some time it was claimed that this species would breed only in clean water, but it has been found that it is not nearly so particular, some even claiming that it prefers foul water. I have seen them breeding in countless thousands in company with *Stegomyia scutellaris* and *Culex fatigans* in the sewer drains in Tahiti in the streets of

Papeete. As the larva feed largely on bacteria one would expect to find them in exactly such places where the bacteria are of course abundant. The fact that they are able to live in any kind of water and in a very small amount of it well adapts them to their habits of living about dwellings.

13. Why does the author list the amounts of different species of organisms in paragraph 1?
    a) To illustrate the vast number of species in the world.
    b) To demonstrate authority on the subject of insects.
    c) To establish the relative importance of mollusks and birds.
    d) To demonstrate the proportion of insects to other organisms.

14. What does the author use "their proper place" at the beginning of paragraph 3?
    a) The author is alluding to people's tendency to view insects as largely irrelevant to their lives.
    b) The author feels that insects belong only outdoors.
    c) The author wants the reader to feel superior to insects.
    d) The author is warning that insects can evolve to affect the course of human events.

15. This passage can be characterized primarily as:
    a) Pedantic.
    b) Droll.
    c) Informative.
    d) Abstract.
    e) Cautionary.

16. The main idea of this passage is best summarized as:
    a) Disease-carrying mosquitoes have adapted to best live near human settlements.
    b) Insects can have a detrimental effect on the economy by destroying crops.
    c) Insects are numerous in both types of species and individuals within a species.
    d) Although people do not always consider insects consequential, they can have substantial effects on human populations.

17. The use of "domestic" in Paragraph 5 most nearly means:
    a) Originating in the United States.
    b) Under the care of and bred by humans.
    c) Fearful of the outdoors.
    d) Living near human homes.

18. Which of the following ideas would best belong in this passage?
    a) An historical example of the effect a yellow fever outbreak had on civilization.
    b) A biological explanation of how diseases are transmitted from insects to humans.
    c) A reference to the numbers of insects which live far away from human habitation.
    d) Strategies for the prevention of yellow fever and malaria.

Questions 19 – 26 are based on a long original passage (author Elissa Yeates):

The collapse of the arbitrage[3] firm Long-Term Capital Management (LTCM) in 1998 is explained by a host of different factors: its investments were based on a high level of leverage, for example, and it was significantly impacted by Russia's default on the ruble. However, sociologist Donald MacKenzie maintains that the main factor in LTCM's demise was that, like all arbitrage firms, it was subjected to the sociological phenomena of the arbitrage community; namely, imitation. Arbitrageurs, who are generally known to one another as members of a specific subset of the financial society, use decision-making strategies based not only on mathematical models or pure textbook reason, but also based upon their feelings and gut reactions toward the financial market and on the actions of their peers. This imitation strategy leads to the overlapping "super portfolio," which creates an inherent instability that leads to collapse, the most infamous example being LTCM.

The public opinion of the partners of the firm in 1998 was that it had acted cavalierly with borrowed capital. However, in actuality the firm's strategy was exceedingly conservative, with a diversified portfolio, overestimated risks, and carefully hedged investments. The firm even tested tactics for dealing with financial emergencies such as the collapse of the European Monetary Union. Before the 1998 crisis, those in LTCM were never accused of recklessness. Nor were they, as is sometimes explained, overly reliant on mathematical models. The statistical hubris explanation falters under MacKenzie's evidence that John Meriwether and the others who ran the firm made their investment decisions based more upon their intricate understandings of the arbitrage market rather than upon the pure results of mathematical analyses. The financial instability that was created was not the result of the decision-making of one firm; but rather, the collective patterns of decision-making of all of the arbitrage firms at the time.

The infamy of LTCM worked against the company. LTCM was composed of some of the most eminent minds in finance and it made devastating profits for the first few years that it was running. This led to imitation by other arbitrageurs who viewed the investments of LTCM as nearly sure bets. This type of replication of investment portfolios is not surprising, considering that arbitrageurs are all looking for similar types of pricing discrepancies and anomalies to exploit. The structure of arbitrageurs as a unique subset of the financial community who are largely personally known to one another further contributes to this phenomenon. Because of these factors over time the various players in the field of arbitrage created overlapping investments which MacKenzie dubs a "super portfolio." While LTCM alone may have created a geographically and industrially diverse portfolio, across the discipline of arbitrage as a whole capital flocked to similar investments.

Because of this super portfolio trend, multiple arbitrageurs were affected by the price changes of different assets caused by the actions of single independent firms. MacKenzie cites the example of the takeover of the investment bank Salomon Brothers by the Travelers Corporation. Salomon Brothers' portfolio, now under the management of someone who disliked the risks of arbitrage trading, liquidated its positions, which drove down the prices of assets in the markets in which it operated. The liquidation of the holdings of such a prominent player in the arbitrage game negatively affected the positions of every other firm that had a stake in those markets, including, of course, LTCM. This also illustrates the other sociological side of MacKenzie's argument: that arbitrageurs are subject to irrational internal pressures to cut their losses before their investments play out, which one of his interview subjects terms "queasiness" when faced with a stretch of losses.

---

[3] "Arbitrage" is a financial strategy which takes advantage of the temporary price differences of a single asset in different markets.

19. The second paragraph of this passage primarily aims to:
   a) Explain that recklessness with borrowed capital is never profitable.
   b) Explore the factors ultimately responsible for the demise of the arbitrage firm Long-Term Capital Management.
   c) Demonstrate how the practice of arbitrage works.
   d) Laud the use of statistical models in calculating financial risks.
   e) Present and dismiss several theories of the collapse of Long-Term Capital Management.

20. In paragraph 2, "devastating" is used to mean:
   a) Destructive.
   b) Attractive.
   c) Blasphemous.
   d) Considerable.
   e) Appalling.

21. The final paragraph in this passage:
   a) Refutes the argument presented in the second paragraph of the passage.
   b) Gives a logical example of the phenomenon described in the introductory first paragraph of the passage.
   c) Contains an ardent plea against the passage of arbitrage.
   d) Gives a step-by-step account of the demise of Long-Term Capital Management.
   e) Argues that an understanding of sociology is crucial to successful financial practice.

22. Which of the following is a best description of the author's approach to the topic?
   a) Impassioned exposition.
   b) Curious exploration.
   c) Gleeful detection.
   d) Disgusted condemnation.
   e) Serene indifference.

23. Which of the following most accurately summarizes the author's thesis?
   a) If Long-Term Capital Management had developed a superportfolio, it would not have collapsed.
   b) Financial markets are inherently instable because those who participate in them are subject to human faults.
   c) Arbitrage firms should always endeavor to have geographically and industrially diverse investments.
   d) Long-Term Capital Management collapsed because arbitrageurs across the industry were investing in the same things, which caused instability.
   e) Long-Term Capital Management was run by financiers who were reckless and overly dependent on mathematical models, which is why it collapsed.

24. "Hubris" in paragraph 2 most likely means:
   a) Mathematical model.
   b) Reliance.
   c) Arrogance.
   d) Denial.
   e) Mistake.

25. Which of the following facts would undermine the main argument of the passage?
   a) The European Monetary Union was close to collapse in 1998.
   b) Some arbitrage firms steered clear of the practice of superportfolios.
   c) The Travelers Corporation was run by financiers who favored the practice of arbitrage.
   d) Arbitrageurs rarely communicate with one another or get information from the same source.
   e) Mathematical models used in finance in the 1990s were highly reliable.

26. Which of the following supports the argument made in the third paragraph?
   a) A detailed outline of the statistical models used by Long-Term Capital Management to make decisions.
   b) An explanation of how other arbitrage firms were able to learn the tactics practiced by Long-Term Capital Management.
   c) Examples of the differences between different investment portfolios of arbitrage firms.
   d) An outline of sociological theories about decision-making processes.
   e) A map showing the geographical diversity of arbitrage investors.

Questions 27 – 36 are based on a long passage excerpted from Robert Louis Stevenson's classic novel ***Treasure Island*** *(public domain). In this passage, the narrator tells about an old sailor staying at his family's inn.*

He had taken me aside one day and promised me a silver fourpenny on the first of every month if I would only keep my "weather-eye open for a seafaring man with one leg" and let him know the moment he appeared. Often enough when the first of the month came round and I applied to him for my wage, he would only blow through his nose at me and stare me down, but before the week was out he was sure to think better of it, bring me my fourpenny piece, and repeat his orders to look out for "the seafaring man with one leg."

How that personage haunted my dreams, I need scarcely tell you. On stormy nights, when the wind shook the four corners of the house and the surf roared along the cove and up the cliffs, I would see him in a thousand forms, and with a thousand diabolical expressions. Now the leg would be cut off at the knee, now at the hip; now he was a monstrous kind of a creature who had never had but the one leg, and that in the middle of his body. To see him leap and run and pursue me over hedge and ditch was the worst of nightmares. And altogether I paid pretty dear for my monthly fourpenny piece, in the shape of these abominable fancies.

But though I was so terrified by the idea of the seafaring man with one leg, I was far less afraid of the captain himself than anybody else who knew him. There were nights when he took a deal more rum and water than his head would carry; and then he would sometimes sit and sing his wicked, old, wild sea-songs, minding nobody; but sometimes he would call for glasses round and force all the trembling company to listen to his stories or bear a chorus to his singing. Often I have heard the house shaking with "Yo-ho-ho, and a bottle of rum," all the neighbors joining in for dear life, with the fear of death upon them, and each singing louder than the other to avoid remark. For in these fits he was the most overriding companion ever known; he would slap his hand on the table for silence all round; he would fly up in a passion of anger at a question, or sometimes because none was put, and so he judged the company was not following his story. Nor would he allow anyone to leave the inn till he had drunk himself sleepy and reeled off to bed.

His stories were what frightened people worst of all. Dreadful stories they were—about hanging, and walking the plank, and storms at sea, and the Dry Tortugas, and wild deeds and places on the Spanish Main. By his own account he must have lived his life among some of the wickedest men that God ever allowed upon the sea, and the language in which he told these stories shocked our plain country people almost as much as the crimes that he described. My father was always saying the inn would be ruined, for people would soon cease coming there to be tyrannized over and put down, and sent shivering to their beds; but I really believe his presence did us good. People were frightened at the time, but on looking back they rather liked it; it was a fine excitement in a quiet country life, and there was even a party of the younger men who pretended to admire him, calling him a "true sea-dog" and a "real old salt" and such like names, and saying there was the sort of man that made England terrible at sea.

In one way, indeed, he bade fair to ruin us, for he kept on staying week after week, and at last month after month, so that all the money had been long exhausted, and still my father never plucked up the heart to insist on having more. If ever he mentioned it, the captain blew through his nose so loudly that you might say he roared, and stared my poor father out of the room. I have seen him wringing his hands after such a rebuff, and I am sure the annoyance and the terror he lived in must have greatly hastened his early and unhappy death.

27. The purpose of Paragraph 3 is to:
    a) Illustrate how others view the captain.
    b) Explain the narrator's relationship with the captain.
    c) Give more background information about the inn where the narrator lives.
    d) Recount old seafaring lore.
    e) Explain why the captain is staying at this inn.

28. Which paragraph serves to evoke the life lived by sailors at sea?
    a) 1.
    b) 2.
    c) 3.
    d) 4.
    e) 5.

29. "Diabolical" in Paragraph 2 most nearly means:
    a) Angry.
    b) Judgmental.
    c) Contorted.
    d) Fiendish.
    e) Stoic.

30. What kind of character does the author reveal the captain to be the third paragraph?
    a) Temperamental.
    b) Generous.
    c) Jocund.
    d) Mysterious.
    e) Reserved.

31. What does the author reveal about the narrator in Paragraph 5?
 a) The narrator is afraid of the captain.
 b) The narrator is eager to go to sea.
 c) The narrator was often angry and annoyed.
 d) The narrator grew up in poverty.
 e) The narrator lost his father at an early age.

32. "Tyrannized" in Paragraph 4 is used to mean:
 a) Cajoled.
 b) Bullied.
 c) Frightened.
 d) Robbed.
 e) Ejected.

33. Which of the following statements about this passage is false?
 a) It is unclear whether the "seafaring man with one leg" actually exists.
 b) The narrator harbors a serious grudge against the captain.
 c) The narrator is interested in the captain's stories.
 d) The story takes place near the ocean.
 e) Most people who populate the story are afraid of the captain.

34. According to the captain, all of the following are hazards which can be encountered at sea EXCEPT:
 a) Hangings.
 b) Wicked men.
 c) Walking the plank.
 d) Storms.
 e) Sea monsters.

35. It can be inferred from the passage that:
 a) Singing was frowned upon in the community.
 b) The narrator never knew his mother.
 c) The narrator admired the captain.
 d) The captain is afraid of the seafaring man with one leg.
 e) The narrator went on to become a pirate.

36. By "they rather liked it" at the end of Paragraph 4, the author most closely means:
 a) The patrons of the inn enjoyed singing.
 b) The captain and others appreciated the rum available for sale at the inn.
 c) The narrator and his friends liked the stories the captain told.
 d) The captain provided entertainment at the inn, which would otherwise be boring.
 e) The narrator's parents liked having the captain around.

*Questions 37 – 40 are based on a short passage excerpted from the introduction to **The Best American Humorous Short Stories**, edited by Alexander Jessup (public domain).*

No book is duller than a book of jokes, for what is refreshing in small doses becomes nauseating when perused in large assignments. Humor in literature is at its best not when served merely by itself but when presented along with other ingredients of literary force in order to give a wide representation of life. Therefore "professional literary humorists," as they may be called, have not been much considered in making up this collection. In the history of American humor there are three names which stand out more prominently than all others before Mark Twain, who, however, also belongs to a wider classification: "Josh Billings" (Henry Wheeler Shaw, 1815-1885), "Petroleum V. Nasby" (David Ross Locke, 1833-1888), and "Artemus Ward" (Charles Farrar Browne, 1834-1867). In the history of American humor these names rank high; in the field of American literature and the American short story they do not rank so high. I have found nothing of theirs that was first-class both as humor and as short story. Perhaps just below these three should be mentioned George Horatio Derby (1823-1861), author of *Phoenixiana* (1855) and the *Squibob Papers* (1859), who wrote under the name "John Phoenix." As has been justly said, "Derby, Shaw, Locke and Browne carried to an extreme numerous tricks already invented by earlier American humorists, particularly the tricks of gigantic exaggeration and calm-faced mendacity, but they are plainly in the main channel of American humor, which had its origin in the first comments of settlers upon the conditions of the frontier, long drew its principal inspiration from the differences between that frontier and the more settled and compact regions of the country, and reached its highest development in Mark Twain, in his youth a child of the American frontier, admirer and imitator of Derby and Browne, and eventually a man of the world and one of its greatest humorists."

37. The author of this passage would disagree with all of the following statements EXCEPT:
   a) To be a successful storyteller, one must also be a professional literary humorist.
   b) Mark Twain is the most prominent American humorist.
   c) Lying with a straight face is a literary humorist device which had just been invented at the time this was published.
   d) The best joke books are the longest ones.
   e) Professional literary humorism is the highest form of writing.

38. The purpose of this passage is to:
   a) Scorn humorous writing as lesser than storytelling.
   b) Explain how writers use humorous literary devices.
   c) Provide contextual information about the landscape of American humorous writing.
   d) Make a case for the appreciation of the humorists Henry Shaw and David Locke.
   e) Deny the historical roots of American literary humor.

39. The word "prominently" in line four most closely means:
   a) Extravagantly.
   b) Inconspicuously.
   c) Significantly.
   d) Comically.
   e) Conceitedly.

40. Which of the following best summarizes the author's theory of the origins of American humorous writing?
   a) It started as a way of breaking away from British literary humor.
   b) It grew hand-in-hand with American storytelling.
   c) It was founded by Mark Twain.
   d) It was inspired by the differences between settlements and the frontier.
   e) It began with exaggerations and mendacity.

1. b)	21. b)
2. c)	22. b)
3. d)	23. d)
4. c)	24. c)
5. a)	25. d)
6. e)	26. b)
7. e)	27. a)
8. a)	28. d)
9. c)	29. d)
10. e)	30. a)
11. a)	31. e)
12. c)	32. b)
13. d)	33. b)
14. a)	34. e)
15. c)	35. c)
16. d)	36. d)
17. d)	37. b)
18. a)	38. c)
19. e)	39. c)
20. d)	40. d)

Chapter 2: Writing Skills

The knowledge just covered in the Reading Placement chapter of this book will come in handy during this section as well. In the Writing Skills portion of the exam, you will need to demonstrate your competency in both the usage and mechanics of the English language, as well as rhetorical skills.

The **usage/mechanics questions** cover the following concepts:

- **Punctuation:** Apostrophes, colons, semi-colons, commas, dashes, hyphens, quotation marks, parentheses, and their functions in clarifying the meaning of text selections.

- **Basic Grammar:** Verbs, adverbs, adjectives, subject-verb agreement, pronoun-antecedent agreement, and the proper use of connectives.

- **Sentence Structure:** Clauses, modifiers, parallelism, consistency in tense, and point-of-view.

Remember the Reading Placement section? The **rhetorical questions** are quite similar. You will be given a passage to read, with questions covering either the entire passage, or separate parts. You will demonstrate your knowledge of:

- **Strategy:** The author's choice of supporting material – if is it effective, applicable, and ample in quality and quantity.

- **Style:** The best choice of adjectives, word order, or alternative wording that most concisely articulates an idea.

- **Organization:** Sentence arrangement within a paragraph, paragraph arrangement within the passage, the need for further information, and the presence of unnecessary information.

Tips

As with all the section tests, you have to know your English grammar. This exam will not be unjustly 'sneaky,' but you do have to be observant and thorough enough to catch errors. Here are some tips to help improve your score.

The Three Main No-No's.
There are three main things the test is stringent about:

1. **Redundancy** (repetitious text or words).

2. **Irrelevance** (words or ideas not directly or logically associated with the purpose or main idea).

3. **Wordiness** (drawing out a sentence).

Peruse the entire passage paragraph before answering any of the questions.

Many study guides will tell you not to read the entire passage before answering the usage/mechanics questions; however, that approach lends to a greater possibility of error. The overall meaning or purpose of the paragraph can change the propriety of the highlighted text. For example, looking at just the sentence containing the highlighted word group may cause you to misinterpret the intended parallels or point of view.

Read every word of every question.
Don't assume that you know what is being asked after reading the first few words. Remember, one word at the end of a sentence can change the entire meaning.

Read all the answer choices before making a selection.
Some choices will be partially correct (pertaining to a part, but not all, of the passage) and are intended to catch the eye of the sloppy tester. Note the differences between your answer choices; sometimes they are very subtle.

Understand transitions.
The exam will require you to recognize the shortest, most proper way to go from one sentence or paragraph to another.

Familiarize yourself with various styles of writing.
The passages may be excerpts from anything: poetry, cause/effect essays, comparison /contrast essays, definition essays, description essays, narration essays, persuasive essays, or process analysis essays.

Learn the directions.
Knowing the directions before test day saves valuable minutes. It enables you to glance quickly at the directions and start answering questions.

And, most importantly, review! Most people cannot learn sentence rules by memorization, like they do math or science. Instead, the best way to learn how sentences fit together is by reading! Studying the following terms and rules will help a great deal.

Syntax

"Syntax" refers to the rules for the formation of grammatical sentences in a language. (That definition, while correct, is pretty stuffy. Basically, "syntax" means "sentence structure.")

It's very easy to understand why syntax is important. In order to convey meaningful information in a way that makes sense, sentences need to comply with the rules of grammar. Most readers and speakers have a general understanding of these rules; it's crucial for you to demonstrate syntactical competency as well.

Let's look at an example.

> "When Heidi woke up in the morning, she noticed three things which disturbed her greatly: the first being that she was a ghost."

But what if we started the sentence this way?

"The first being that she was a ghost: she noticed three things when Heidi woke up which disturbed her greatly."

After reading this sentence, you would probably be utterly confused and, most likely, unwilling to continue reading. Why would you have this reaction? Because the sentence doesn't make grammatical sense.

Now the above example is very easy. But chances are that the questions on the exam may be a bit harder. Therefore, it's important that you understand the top five grammatical rules:

1. Sentences that maintain the subject-verb-object order are more readable than those which do not.

2. When you can, place the subject and the verb close together in a sentence.

3. Keep modifiers and the words that they modify close together in a sentence.

4. Try to put people in the subject position in a sentence.

5. Put old information first in a sentence and new information last.

Nouns, Pronouns, Verbs, Adjectives, and Adverbs

Nouns
Nouns are people, places, or things. They are typically the subject of a sentence. For example, "The hospital was very clean." The noun is "hospital;" it is the "place."

Pronouns
Pronouns essentially "replace" nouns. This allows a sentence to not sound repetitive. Take the sentence: "Sam stayed home from school because Sam was not feeling well." The word "Sam" appears twice in the same sentence. Instead, you can use a pronoun and say, "Sam stayed at home because *he* did not feel well." Sounds much better, right?

Most Common Pronouns:

- I, me, mine, my.

- You, your, yours.

- He, him, his.

- She, her, hers.

- It, its.

- We, us, our, ours.

36

- They, them, their, theirs.

Verbs

Remember the old commercial, "Verb: It's what you do"? That sums up verbs in a nutshell! Verbs are the "action" of a sentence; verbs "do" things.

They can, however, be quite tricky. Depending on the subject of a sentence, the tense of the word (past, present, future, etc.), and whether or not they are regular or irregular, verbs have many variations.

Example: "He runs to second base." The verb is "runs." This is a "regular verb."

Example: "I am 7 years old." The verb in this case is "am." This is an "irregular verb."

As mentioned, verbs must use the correct tense – and that tense must remain the same throughout the sentence. "I was baking cookies and eat some dough." That sounded strange, didn't it? That's because the two verbs "baking" and "eat" are presented in different tenses. "Was baking" occurred in the past; "eat," on the other hand, occurs in the present. Instead, it should be "**ate** some dough."

Adjectives

Adjectives are words that describe a noun and give more information. Take the sentence: "The boy hit the ball." If you want to know more about the noun "boy," then you could use an adjective to describe it. "The **little** boy hit the ball." An adjective simply provides more information about a noun or subject in a sentence.

Adverbs

For some reason, many people have a difficult time with adverbs – but don't worry! They are really quite simple. Adverbs are similar to adjectives in that they provide more information; however, they describe verbs, adjectives, and even other adverbs. They do **not** describe nouns – that's an adjective's job.

Take the sentence: "The doctor said she hired a new employee."

It would give more information to say: "The doctor said she **recently** hired a new employee." Now we know more about *how* the action was executed. Adverbs typically describe when or how something has happened, how it looks, how it feels, etc.

Good vs. Well

A very common mistake that people make concerning adverbs is the misuse of the word "good."

"Good" is an adjective – things taste good, look good, and smell good. "Good" can even be a noun – "Superman does good" – when the word is speaking about "good" vs. "evil." HOWEVER, "good" is never an adverb.

People commonly say things like, "I did really good on that test," or, "I'm good." Ugh! This is NOT the correct way to speak! In those sentences, the word "good" is being used to describe an action: how a person **did**, or how a person **is**. Therefore, the adverb "well" should be used. "I did really **well** on that test." "I'm **well**."

The correct use of "well" and "good" can make or break a person's impression of your grammar – make sure to always speak correctly!

Study Tips for Improving Vocabulary and Grammar

1. You're probably pretty computer savvy and know the Internet very well. Visit the Online Writing Lab website, which is sponsored by Purdue University, at http://owl.english.purdue.edu. This site provides you with an excellent overview of syntax, writing style, and strategy. It also has helpful and lengthy review sections that include multiple-choice "Test Your Knowledge" quizzes, which provide immediate answers to the questions.

2. It's beneficial to read the entire passage first to determine its intended meaning BEFORE you attempt to answer any questions. Doing so provides you with key insight into a passage's syntax (especially verb tense, subject-verb agreement, modifier placement, writing style, and punctuation).

3. When you answer a question, use the "Process-of-Elimination Method" to determine the best answer. Try each of the four answers and determine which one BEST fits with the meaning of the paragraph. Find the BEST answer. Chances are that the BEST answer is the CORRECT answer.

Directions:

This test consists of four passages. In each passage, certain words and phrases have been underlined and numbered. The questions on each passage consist of alternatives for these underlined segments. Choose the alternative that follows standard written English, most accurately reflects the style and tone of the passage, or best relays the idea of the passage. Choose "No Change" if no change is necessary.

You are to choose the best answer to the question.

You will also find questions about a section of the passage, or the passage as a whole. These questions do not refer to the underlined portions of the passage, but are identified by a boxed number. For each question, choose the alternative that best answers the question.

PASSAGE I: Examining my Ecological Footprint

Examining the impact my lifestyle has on the earth's resources is <u>a fascinating and</u>
1
<u>valuable thing to do</u>. According to the Earth Day Network ecological footprint calculator created by the Sierra Club, it would take four planet earths to sustain the human population if everyone used as many resources as I do. My "ecological footprint," or the amount of productive area of the earth that is required to produce the resources I consume, <u>must then be much</u> larger
2

<u>like those of</u> most of the population.
3
It is hard to balance the luxuries and opportunities I have available to <u>me: with</u> doing what I know to be
4
better from an ecological standpoint.

One's ecological footprint is <u>measured with</u>
5
accounting for different factors such as how often and how far one drives and travels by air, what kind of structure one lives in, and what kind of goods one consumes (and how far those consumer goods travel

1.

    a) NO CHANGE
    b) a fascinating or valuable thing to do.
    c) fascinating to do and also valuable to do.
    d) done to be fascinating or valuable.

2.

    f) NO CHANGE
    g) would have been
    h) much
    j) was much

3.

    a) NO CHANGE
    b) than those of
    c) than footprints of
    d) as the footprints of

4.

    f) NO CHANGE
    g) me, with
    h) me; with
    j) me with

5.

    a) NO CHANGE
    b) measured by
    c) measured with
    d) measured of

across the globe). For example, a person who lives in a freestanding home, which uses more energy to heat and cool than an apartment in a building does; who travels internationally several times per year; and who eats exotic, out-of-season foods which must be shipped in from other countries, rather than locally grown and raised food <u>which is</u> in season,

6

would have a large ecological footprint.

<u>7</u>

Although I get points for recycling, <u>my use of</u> public transportation, and living in an

8

apartment complex rather than a free-standing residence; my footprint expands when it is taken into account my not-entirely-local diet, my occasional use of a car, my three magazine subscriptions, and my history of flying more than ten hours a year. These are all examples of things that use a large amount of resources.

<u>9</u>

6.
   f) NO CHANGE
   g) that are
   h) those are
   j) which are

7. The last sentence in the above paragraph could be improved by:

   a) Being broken into short sentences.
   b) Being moved to the beginning of the paragraph.
   c) Including information about how the footprint is calculated.
   d) Taking out "for example" at the beginning of the sentence.

8.
   f) NO CHANGE
   g) use of
   h) using
   j) my using

9. The writer wants to add a sentence to the end of the paragraph that encourages others to calculate their own ecological footprint. Which of the following sentences would best accomplish this?

   a) There are many different ways that we use resources that may be surprising.
   b) Other things I do that use high amounts of resources include using a dryer for my laundry and leaving appliances plugged in when I'm out of the house.
   c) Sources of waste are often surprising; you can calculate your own ecological footprint online at myfootprint.org.

This examination of the impact my lifestyle <u>has</u>

<u>on the earth's resources</u> is fascinating and valuable
10

to me. It is fairly easy for me to recycle, so I do it,

but it would be much harder to <u>forgoing</u> the
11

opportunity to travel by plane or eat my favorite

<u>fruits; that</u> have been flown to the supermarket from
12

a different country. I feel that realizing just how

unfair my share of the <u>earths' resources has</u> been
13

should help me to change at least some of my bad

habit. Perhaps if we were all made aware of the true

cost of our habits, actions, and <u>choices, people</u>
14

would be more likely to take steps to reduce <u>his or</u>
15

<u>her</u> consumption of the earth's resources.

d) Sometimes the best way to reduce one's use of resources is to travel less.

10.
f) NO CHANGE
g) on the resources of the planet
h) had on the earth's resources
j) has on the earth resources

11.
a) NO CHANGE
b) forgo
c) have forgone
d) not forgo

12.
f) NO CHANGE
g) fruits, that
h) fruits that
j) fruits: that

13.
a) NO CHANGE
b) earth's resources has
c) earths' resources have
d) earth's resources have

14.
f) NO CHANGE
g) choices. People
h) choices; people
j) than people

15.
a) NO CHANGE
b) our
c) their
d) one's

PASSAGE II
The Sculptor Augusta Savage

Augusta <u>Savage were</u> a world-famous African-
         16
American sculptor. <u>Born in Florida,</u> her first formal
                    17
art training was in New York City at Cooper Union,

the school recommended to her by Solon Gorglum.

<u>While she studied,</u> she supported herself by doing
         18
odd jobs, including clerking and working in

laundries. In 1926 she exhibited her work at the

Sesquicentennial Exposition in Philadelphia. That

same year she was awarded a scholarship to study in

Rome. However, she was unable to accept the

award because she could not raise the money <u>she</u>

<u>would have needed</u> to live there.
         19

When she returned to the United States, she

exhibited her work at several important galleries. <u>In</u>

<u>addition to her own work,</u> Augusta Savage taught
                    20
art classes in Harlem. During the Depression, she

helped African- American artists to enroll in the

Works Progress Administration arts project.

Throughout her career, she was an active

spokesperson for African-American artists in the

United <u>States. She also</u> was one of the principal

16.
- f) NO CHANGE
- g) Savage, was
- h) Savage, were
- j) Savage was

17.
- a) NO CHANGE
- b) She was born in Florida,
- c) While being born inFlorida,
- d) Although she was born in Florida,

18.
- f) NO CHANGE
- g) While she studied
- h) After studying
- j) She studied while

19.
- a) NO CHANGE
- b) she would need
- c) she needed
- d) she needs

20.
- f) NO CHANGE
- g) Additional to creating her own work,
- h) Additionally to her own work,
- j) In addition to creating her own work,

21
organizers of the Harlem Artists Guild.

In <u>1923 Savage,</u> applied for a summer art
     22

program sponsored by the French government;

despite being more than qualified, she was turned

down by the international judging committee, solely

because of her race. Savage was deeply upset,

<u>questioning</u> the committee, beginning the first of
   23

many public fights for equal rights in her life. The

incident got press coverage on both sides of the

Atlantic, and eventually the sole supportive

committee member, sculptor Hermon Atkins

MacNeil—who at one time had shared a studio with

Henry Ossawa Tanner—<u>invited her to study with</u>
                24

<u>him</u>.

She later <u>cite</u> him as one of her teachers.
   25

In 1939, Augusta Savage received a

commission from the World's Fair and created a 16

foot tall plaster sculpture called *Lift Ev'ry Voice*

and Sing. Savage did not have any funds for a

bronze cast, or even to move and store <u>it</u>, and it was
                      26

destroyed by bulldozers at the close of the fair.

However, small metal and plaster souvenir copies of

21. The author wants to combine the last two sentences of this paragraph. What is the best way to rewrite the underlined portion?

  a) States; she also
  b) States, although she also
  c) States, and also
  d) States and she

22.
  f) NO CHANGE
  g) 1923 Savage
  h) 1923, Savage
  j) 1923; Savage

23.
  a) NO CHANGE
  b) and questioned
  c) and questioning
  d) and so she questioned

24.
  f) NO CHANGE
  g) invited her to study with himself
  h) invited him to study with her
  j) gave her an invitation to study with him

25.
  a) NO CHANGE
  b) was citing
  c) citing
  d) cited

26.
  f) NO CHANGE
  g) the plaster
  h) them
  j) her

the sculpture <u>has</u> survived.
27

28

Perhaps Savage's more indelible legacy is the work of the students whom she taught in her studio, the Savage Studio of Arts and Crafts. Her students included Jacob Lawrence, Norman Lewis, and Gwendolyn Knight. Lawrence was a Cubist painter whose work is hosted in museums across the country. Lewis was an Abstract Expressionist painter who often dealt with music and jazz in abstract ways. <u>Knight who was born in Barbados</u>
29
founded an organization to support young artists. Augusta Savage <u>worked tireless</u> to teach these
30
artists, help them to secure funding, and support their careers.

27.
   a) NO CHANGE
   b) have
   c) were
   d) would

28. Which sentence would best fit at the beginning of the paragraph that now begins "In 1939"?

   f) Her education in the arts was substantial after working with so many high profit sculptors.
   g) African-Americans were still facing terrible discrimination at the end of the 1930's.
   h) The World's Fair is a huge art exhibit that occurs every two to four years.
   j) Throughout the 1930's, her profile as an artist continued to grow.

29.
   a) NO CHANGE
   b) Knight, who was born in Barbados
   c) Knight who was born in Barbados,
   d) Knight, who was born in Barbados,

30.
   f) NO CHANGE
   g) worked tirelessly
   h) worked herself tireless
   j) was working tireless

PASSAGE III
History of Art for Beginners and Students – Ancient Painting

The following passage is adapted from Clara Erskine Clément's History of Art for Beginners and Students, first published in 1887 (public domain; errors inserted for the purposes of crafting questions).

In speaking of art we often contrast the useful or mechanical arts with the Fine Arts; by these terms we denote the difference between the arts which are used in making such things as are necessary and useful in civilized life, and the arts by which ornamental and beautiful things made. The fine
31
arts are Architecture, Sculpture, Painting, Poetry, and Music, and though we could live if none of these existed, yet life would be far from the pleasant
32
experience that it is often made to be through the
33
enjoyment of these arts.

Of course, forms of art can be both fine and useful. While painting belongs to the fine or beautiful arts, it is a very useful art in many ways. For example, when a school-book is illustrated, how much more easily we understand the subject we are studying through the help we get from pictures of objects or places that we have not otherwise seen. Pictures of natural scenery bring all countries before our eyes in such a way that by looking at it, while
34

31.
a) NO CHANGE
b) things.
c) things are made.
d) things are used.

32.
f) NO CHANGE
g) existed,
h) yet,
j) existed and yet

33.
a) NO CHANGE
b) made out to be
c) made
d) is

34.
f) NO CHANGE
g) those
h) them
j) one

reading books of travel, we may know a great deal

more about lands we have never seen, and may

never be able to visit.

35

St. Augustine, who wrote in the fourth century,
                                                    36
says that "pictures are the books of the simple or

unlearned." This is just as true now as then, and we

should regard pictures as one of the best methods

for teaching. The cultivation of the

imagination is very important because for this way
                        37
we can add much to our individual happiness. Thus

one of the uses of pictures is that they give us a

clear idea of what we have not seen; a second use is

that they are exciting to our imaginations, and often
          38
help us to forget disagreeable circumstances and

unpleasant surroundings. Through this power, if we

are in a dark, narrow street, in a house which is not

to our liking, or in the midst of any unpleasant
                    39
happenings, we are able to fix our thoughts upon a

photograph or picture that may be there, and

we are able to imagine ourselves far, far

away, in some spot where nature makes everything

pleasant and soothes us into forgetfulness of all that

makes us unhappy. Many an invalid—many

an unfortunate person is made content by pictures

35. Which of the following sentences could be added to the above paragraph to give another example of how pictures are useful as well as decorative?

   a) Pictures are not useful, however, when they distract students from the purpose of a text.
   b) Pictures can be a beautiful addition to our homes.
   c) Doctors often use pictures when studying the body to help them learn organs and systems.
   d) This is helpful because people really don't travel to other lands anymore.

36.
   f) NO CHANGE
   g) century says
   h) century said
   j) century, said

37.
   a) NO CHANGE
   b) important, because in
   c) important, because for
   d) important; in

38.
   f) NO CHANGE
   g) exciting
   h) excite
   j) excited

39. If the writer deletes this section of this sentence, what will be lost?

   a) Nothing; the meaning of the sentence will not change.
   b) The argument that pictures are useful.
   c) The example of pictures being educational.
   d) The generalization of the specific example to all unpleasant circumstances.

47

during hours that would <u>otherwise be</u> wretched.
40
This is the result of cultivating the <u>imagination and</u>

<u>when</u> this is done, we have a source of pleasure
41
within ourselves which can never be taken from

us.

 It often happens that we see two people <u>doing</u>
           42
the same work and are situated in the same way in

the world, but who are different in their <u>manner</u>
           43
<u>one</u> is light-hearted and happy, the other sullen and

sad. If you can find out the truth, it will be that

the sad one is matter-of-fact, and has no

imagination—he can only think of his work and

what concerns him personally; but the merry one

would surprise you if you could read his thoughts—

if you could know the distances <u>they have</u> passed
          44
over, and what a vast difference there is between his

thought and his work. So while it is natural for

almost everyone to exclaim <u>joyful</u> at the beauty of
         45
pictures, and to enjoy looking at them simply, I

wish my readers to think of their uses also, and

understand the benefits that may be derived from

them.

40.
 f) NO CHANGE
 g) tend to be
 h) however be
 j) be

41.
 a) NO CHANGE
 b) imagination so when
 c) imagination, and when
 d) imagination; when

42.
 f) NO CHANGE
 g) are doing
 h) who do
 j) done

43.
 a) NO CHANGE
 b) manner; one
 c) manner. One
 d) manner: one

44.
 f) NO CHANGE
 g) he has
 h) it has
 j) you have

45.
 a) NO CHANGE
 b) joyfully
 c) joy
 d) with joy

1. a)

2. f)

3. b)

4. j)

5. b)

6. f)

7. a)

8. h) This is an instance of parallelism, where you want verbs in a list in a sentence to have the same form.

9. c)

10. f)

11. b)

12. h)

13. b)

14. f)

15. c)

16. j)

17. d) This is an example of a misplaced modifier and needs to be edited.

18. f)

19. a)

20. j)

21. c)

22. h)

23. b)

24. f)

25. d)

26. g)

27. b)

28. j) This sentence best follows the topic of the passage while leading into the new information in this paragraph.

29. d)

30. g)

31. c)

32. g)

33. d)

34. h)

35. c)

36. f)

37. b)

38. h)

39. d)

40. f)

41. c)

42. h)

43. d)

44. f)

45. b)

Chapter 3: Writing Essay

Now that you have refreshed your reading comprehension and sentence skills, we can move onto the essay portion of the exam. By combining all of the knowledge gained in the previous chapters, as well as the information covered in this chapter, you can effectively create a high-quality piece of work!

Your essay will either be graded on a 2 – 8 (with 8 being the highest score possible) or 8 – 12 (with 12 being the highest score possible) scale. This overall score will be broken down into the sub-scores of: focus, content, organization, style, and conventions.

An Effective Essay Demonstrates:

1. Insightful and effective development of a point-of-view on the issue.

2. Critical thinking skills. For example: Two oppositions are given; instead of siding with one, you provide examples in which both would be appropriate.

3. Organization. It is clearly focused and displays a smooth progression of ideas.

4. Supportive information. If a statement is made, it is followed by examples, reasons, or other supporting evidence.

5. Skillful use of varied, accurate, and apt vocabulary.

6. Sentence variety. (Not every sentence follows a "subject-verb" pattern. Mix it up!)

7. Proper grammar and spelling.

Things to Keep in Mind While Writing Your Essay

- **Rhetorical Force**: This factor judges how coherently the writer composes their essay. How clear is the idea or argument that is being presented?

- **Organization**: The writing must have a logical order, so that the reader can easily follow along and understand the main points being made.

- **Support and Development**: The use and quality of supporting arguments and information. Essays should not be vague.

- **Usage**: Essays should demonstrate a competent command of word choice, showing both accuracy and quality in the words used.

- **Structure and Convention**: Essays should be free of errors, including: spelling, punctuation, capitalization, sentence structure, etc.

- **Appropriateness**: Essays should be written in a style appropriate for the topic; they should also contain material appropriate for both the topic and the audience.

- **Timing**: You will have a limited time within which to write your essay. Pace yourself; and practice, practice, practice!

In this chapter, we will provide a sample essay prompt, followed by four short sample responses. The four sample responses each display different qualities of work; an explanation will follow each sample, explaining what score it would have earned and why.

Essay Examples and Evaluations

Prompt:
Research tells us that what children learn in their earliest years is very important to their future success in school. Because of this, public schools all over the country are starting to offer Pre-Kindergarten classes.

What are the benefits of starting school early? What are some of the problems you see in sending four-year-olds to school?

Write a composition in which you weigh the pros and cons of public school education for Pre-Kindergartners. Give reasons and specific examples to support your opinion. There is no specific word limit for your composition, but it should be long enough to give a clear and complete presentation of your ideas.

Sample High-Quality Essay

Today, more and more four-year-olds are joining their big brothers and sisters on the school bus and going to Pre-Kindergarten. Although the benefits of starting school early are clear, it is also clear that Pre-K is not for every child.

The students who are successful in Pre-K are ahead when they start kindergarten. Pre-K teaches them to play well with others. Even though it does not teach skills like reading and writing, it does help to prepare students for "real" school. Pre-K students sing songs, dance, paint and draw, climb and run. They learn to share and to follow directions. They tell stories and answer questions, and as they do, they add new words to their vocabularies. Pre-K can also give students experiences they might not get at home. They might take trips to the zoo or the farm, have visits from musicians or scientists, and so on. These experiences help the students better understand the world.

There are, however, some real differences among children of this age. Some four-year-olds are just not ready for the structure of school life. Some have a hard time leaving home, even for only three or four hours a day. Other children may already be getting a great preschool education at home or in daycare.

While you weigh the advantages and disadvantages of Pre-K, it is safe to say that each child is different. For some children, it is a wonderful introduction to the world of school. But others may not or should not be forced to attend Pre-K.

Evaluation of Sample High-Quality Essay
This paper is clearly organized and has stated a definite point of view. The paper opens with an introduction and closes with a conclusion. The introduction and conclusion combine an expression of the writer's opinion. Connections to the writer's opinion are made throughout the paper.

Sample Medium-Quality Essay

Just like everything in life, there are pros and cons to early childhood education. Pre-K classes work for many children, but they aren't for everyone. The plusses of Pre-K are obvious. Pre-K children learn many skills that will help them in kindergarten and later on. Probably the most important thing they learn is how to follow directions. This is a skill they will need at all stages of their life.

Other plusses include simple tasks like cutting, coloring in the lines, and learning capital letters. Many children don't get these skills at home. They need Pre-K to prepare them for kindergarten.

The minuses of Pre-K are not as obvious, but they are real. Children at this young age need the comfort of home. They need to spend time with parents, not strangers. They need that security. If parents are able to, they can give children the background they need to do well in school.

Other minuses include the fact that a lot of four year-old children can't handle school. They don't have the maturaty to sit still, pay attention, or share with others. Given another year, they may mature enough to do just fine in school. Sometimes it's better just to wait.

So there are definitely good things about Pre-K programs in our public schools, and I would definitely want to see one in our local schools. However, I think parents should decide whether their children are ready for a Pre-K education or not.

Evaluation of Sample Medium-Quality Essay

This paper has an identifiable organization plan, with pros and cons listed in order. The development is easy to understand, if not somewhat simplistic. The language of the paper is uneven, with some vague turns of phrase: "Just like everything in life," "definitely some good things." The word "maturity" is also misspelled. However, the essay is clear and controlled, and generally follows written conventions. If the writer had included more developed and explicit examples and used more varied words, this paper might have earned a higher score.

Sample Low-Quality Essay

What are benefits? What are some of problems with sending four-year-olds to school? Well, for one problem, its hard to see how little kids would do with all those big kids around at the school. They might get bullyed or lern bad habits, so I wouldnt want my four year old around those big kids on the bus and so on. Its hard to see how that could be good for a four year old. In our area we do have Pre-Kindergarten at our school but you dont have to go there a lot of kids in the program, I think about 50 or more, you see them a lot on the play ground mostly all you see them do is play around so its hard to see how that could be too usefull. They could play around at home just as easy. A reason for not doing Pre-Kindergarten is then what do you learn in Kindergarten. Why go do the same thing two years when you could just do one year when your a little bit bigger (older). I wonder do the people who want Pre- Kindergarten just want there kids out of the house or a baby sitter for there kids. Its hard to see why do we have to pay for that. I dont even know if Kindergarten is so usefull anyway, not like first grade where you actially learn something. So I would say theres lots of problems with Pre-Kindergarten.

Evaluation of Sample Low-Quality Essay

This paper barely responds to the prompt. It gives reasons not to support Pre-K instruction, but it does not present any benefits of starting school early. The writer repeats certain phrases ("It's hard to see") to no real effect, and the faulty spelling, grammar, and punctuation significantly impede understanding. Several sentences wander off the topic entirely ("there a lot of kids in the program, I think about 50 or more, you see them a lot on the playground.", "I dont even know if Kindergarten is so usefull anyway, not like first grade where you actially learn something."). Instead of opening with an introduction, the writer simply lifts phrases from the prompt. The conclusion states the writer's opinion, but the reasons behind it are illogical and vague. Rather than organizing the essay in paragraph form, the writer has written a single, run-on paragraph. The lack of organization, weak language skills, and failure to address the prompt earn this essay a low score.

Test Your Knowledge: Writing Essay

Prompt One

Provided below is an excerpt and a question. Use the excerpt to prompt your thinking, and then plan and write an essay by answering the question from your perspective. Be sure to provide evidence.

- *General George S. Patton Jr. is quoted as having said, "No good decision was ever made in a swivel chair."*

Is it necessary to be directly in a situation in order to best understand what must be done?

Prompt Two

Provided below is an excerpt and a question. Use the excerpt to prompt your thinking, and then plan and write an essay by answering the question from your perspective. Be sure to provide evidence.

- *In The Dispossessed, published in 1974, groundbreaking science fiction author Ursula K. LeGuin wrote, "You can't crush ideas by suppressing them. You can only crush them by ignoring them."*

Is it possible to get rid of an idea?

Prompt Three

Provided below is an excerpt and a question. Use the excerpt to prompt your thinking, and then plan and write an essay by answering the question from your perspective. Be sure to provide evidence.

- *"The paradox of education is precisely this -- that as one begins to become conscious one begins to examine the society in which he is being educated."* *James Baldwin (1924-1987), American novelist, poet, and social critic*

Does a successful education require the examination of one's own society?

The following pages hold sample scored essays for topics one, two, and three. Look for: reasoning, examples, word usage, coherency, and detail. There are no "right" answers on your essay; the most important factor is that the argument be well developed.

Essays for Prompt One

Is it necessary to be directly in a situation to best understand what must be done?

High Quality:
General George Patton was speaking of war when he noted that "no good decision was ever made in a swivel chair;" however, that observation applies to situations beyond battle. While a big-picture perspective is useful in analyzing situations and deciding how to act, an on-the-ground outlook is essential. In matters of politics, and technology, to name two, the best-laid plans usually have to be changed to respond to changing circumstances.

55

One example which illustrates the necessity of on-the-ground action is the famous space flight of Apollo 13. Before launch, all plans were worked out to get the manned mission to the moon and back. However, due to a fluke set of circumstances – an oxygen tank explosion and the resulting technical problems – the plans had to change. The successful return of Apollo 13 and the survival of its crew would not have been possible without the quick thinking of the men on board. They first noticed the incident, well before the technical crew in Houston would have detected it from Earth. While the work of the technical crew was of course key as well, without the astronauts on board the ship to implement an emergency plan, the mission would surely have been lost.

Just as there are often unforeseen circumstances when implementing technology, politics can also be unpredictable. For example, the Cuban Missile Crisis in 1962 required immediate, on-the-ground decision making by the leaders of the United States. Prior to the Cold War standoff, President Kennedy and his advisors had already decided their hardline position against Soviet weapons expansion in the Western hemisphere. The Monroe Doctrine, status quo since the 1920s, held that European countries should not practice their influence in the Americas. The Soviet Union tested this line by establishing intermediate-range missiles on the island of Cuba. President Kennedy could not simply hold to the established wisdom, because the true limits had never been tested. Instead, to stave off the threat of attack, he was forced to act immediately as events unfolded to preserve the safety of American lives. The crisis unfolded minute-by-minute, with formerly confident advisors unsure of the smartest step. Eventually, after thirteen tense days, the leaders were able to reach a peaceful conclusion.

What these events of the 1960s illustrate is that the best laid plans are often rendered useless by an unfolding situation. For crises to be resolved, whether they be in war, technology, or politics; leaders must have level heads in the moment with up-to-date information. Therefore, plans established in advance by those in swivel chairs with level heads are not always the best plans to follow. History has shown us that we must be able to think on our feet as unforeseen situations unfold.

Medium Quality:
It is often necessary to be directly on the ground as a situation unfolds to know what is best do to. This is because situations can be unpredictable and what you previously

thought was the best course of action, is not always so. This can be seen in the unfolding events of the 1962 Cuban Missile Crisis.

The Cuban Missile Crisis happened in 1962, during the presidency of John F. Kennedy, when Nikita Khrushchev, president of the Soviet Union, developed an intermediate-range missile base on the island of Cuba, within range of the United States. Since the Monroe Doctrine in the 1920s, the United States leaders have declared that they would not tolerate this kind of aggression. However, the decisions that had been made by leaders in the past, removed from the situation, were no longer relevant. It was necessary for President Kennedy to make decisions as events unfolded.

As the Cuban Missile Crisis shows us, at turning points in history decisions have to be made as events unfold by those who are in the middle of a situation. Otherwise, we would all be acting according to what those in the past and those removed from the challenge thought was best. Following the Monroe Doctrine could have resulted in unnecessary violence.

Low Quality:

It is necessary to make decisions while in the middle of a situation, not above the situation, because there is always information that is only known to people in the middle of the situation. For example, in a war, the strategists in Washington might have an overall aim in the war, but they would be unable to know what it best to do on the ground. Situations like running out of ammunition or the enemy having an unexpected backup could change the decisions that need to be made. This was especially true before cell phones and other digital technologies made communication easier.

Essays for Prompt Two

Is it possible to get rid of an idea?

High Quality:

The suppression of ideas has been attempted over and over throughout history by different oppressive regimes. This theme has been explored as well in literature, through such dystopian works as 1984 and Fahrenheit 451. But these histories and stories always play out the same way: eventually, the repressed idea bubbles to the surface and triumphs. Ursula K. LeGuin acknowledged this by saying that ideas can be crushed not by suppression, but by omission.

In Aldous Huxley's novel <u>Brave New World</u>, the world government maintains order not by governing people strictly and policing their ideas, but by distracting them. Consumption is the highest value of the society. When an outsider to the society comes in and questions it, he is exiled – not to punish him, but to remove his influence from society. The government of the dystopia has learned that the best way to maintain control is to keep citizens unaware of other, outside ideas. This theme resonates with a modern audience more than other, more authoritarian tales of dystopia because in our society, we are less controlled than we are influenced and persuaded.

Repressing ideas through harsh authoritarian rule has proven time and again to be ultimately fruitless. For example, in Soviet Russia during the 1920s and 1930s, Josef Stalin attempted to purge his society of all religious belief. This was done through suppression: discriminatory laws were enacted, members of the clergy were executed, and the religious citizenry were terrified. While these measures drastically crippled religious institutions, they were ineffective at completely eliminating the idea of religion. Beliefs and traditions were passed down in communities clandestinely throughout the repressive rule of Stalin. After the fall of the Soviet Union, it became clear that religion had survived all along.

We see throughout literature and history that ignoring ideas and distracting people from them is generally more effective than to attempt to stamp an idea out through means of suppression. Authoritarian rule, in fact, can do the opposite: by dramatizing and calling attention to an idea in the name of condemning it, a regime might actually strengthen that idea.

Medium Quality:

We have seen different governments try to crush out ideas throughout history. However, they are never actually successful in doing so. An idea can be ignored or suppressed, but it will never really go away. This is illustrated in the survival of religion in the Soviet Union.

In Soviet Russia during the 1920s and 1930s, Josef Stalin attempted to purge the society of all religious belief. This was done through suppression: discriminatory laws, execution of the clergy, and use of terror. While this harmed religious institutions, they were ineffective at crushing the idea of religion. Beliefs and traditions were passed down in communities secretly throughout the rule of Stalin. After the fall of the Soviet Union, it became clear that religion had survived all along.

The same kind of thing happened with apartheid law in South Africa. Even though there were laws against black Africans and white Africans using the same facilities, the idea caught fire, especially because of an international outcry against the law.

We see throughout history that suppressing ideas does not crush them. Authoritarian rule, in fact, can do the opposite: by calling attention to an idea in the name of condemning it, a regime might actually strengthen that idea.

Low Quality:

It is not possible to crush out an idea by ignoring it or by suppressing it. All throughout history, whenever anyone has tried to do this, they might be temporarily successful but the idea will always survive or come back. For example in the Soviet Union religion was suppressed. People were not allowed to practice their religion. But after the government fell, religion still existed – people had held on to their ideas during the time of suppression.

Essays for Prompt Three

Does a successful education require the examination of one's own society?

High Quality:

James Baldwin noted that education is a paradox – as one becomes educated, one starts to question the educators. This is necessarily true, because an education is not just a mastery of facts and information but also acquiring the ability to think critically and forge new connections. Progress in society comes from people who understand the thought that came before and are then able to take it one step further. This theme plays out in social activism and in science, for example.

A society's understanding of human rights is constantly evolving. For this process to continue, each generation must question the mores taught by the previous generation. This process can be seen in America in the progression of women's rights, the rights of non-whites, religious rights, and the rights of the disabled. One hundred years ago, these groups had far less constitutional protection than they do today. It takes groups of educated people with a forward-thinking understanding to advocate and press for changes to be made. To take one example, women have gone from not having the right to vote in 1912 to, one hundred years later, women beginning to run for the highest political office. This happened because people like Elizabeth Cady Stanton, a suffragist in the 1850s, and Marsha Griffiths, the Representative in Congress in the 1970s who championed for the Equal Rights Amendment, were able to take the precepts of justice and equality taught to them and take them a step further by applying them to women's rights.

This pattern of taking knowledge a step further can also be seen in the fields of science and mathematics. Sir Isaac Newton, one of the inventors of calculus, is attributed with saying he "stood on the shoulders of giants." He took the concepts well established in mathematics – geometry and algebra – and used the tools in a new way to create calculus. To do this, he had to both already understand what was known in the field but also be able to look at it critically. Without people doing this, fields like science and math would never progress.

A society that is interested in advancing, in rights, science, and every other field, must educate its citizens not to only understand the knowledge of the past but also to criticize prior thought and look at things in a new way. This is what James Baldwin meant – a truly educated person will question everything, even his or her own society, in order to progress.

Medium Quality:

James Baldwin noted that education is a paradox – as one becomes educated, one starts to question the educators. This is true because an education is not just a mastery of facts and information but also ability to think critically and forge new connections. Progress in society comes from people who understand the thought that came before and are then able to take it one step further. One example of this is in human and political rights.

A society's understanding of human rights is constantly evolving. For this process to continue, each generation must question the mores taught by the previous generation. This process can be seen in America in the progression of women's rights, the rights of non-whites, religious rights, and the rights of the disabled. One hundred years ago, these groups had far less constitutional protection than they do today. It takes groups of educated people with a forward-thinking understanding to press for changes to be made. To take one example, women have gone from not having the right to vote in 1912 to, one hundred years later, women beginning to run for the highest political office. This happened because people like Elizabeth Cady Stanton, a suffragist in the 1850s, and Marsha Griffiths, the Representative in Congress in the 1970s who championed for the Equal Rights Amendment, were able to take the precepts of justice and equality taught to them and take them a step further by applying them to women's rights.

A society that is interested in advancing, in rights every other field, must educate its citizens not to only understand the knowledge of the past but also to criticize prior thought and look at things in a new way. This is what James Baldwin meant – a truly educated person will question everything, even his or her own society, in order to progress.

Low Quality:

James Baldwin said that education is a paradox – as one becomes educated, one starts to question the educators. He is right about this, because being educated is not just about knowing the facts. It is also about critical thinking. Without thinking critically about one's own society, then people never make progress. This was necessary for things like civil rights, they could not just accept what was taught in the schools about the rights people should have. Probably the most important part of being educated is questioning the society you live in.

Chapter 4: Math Placement

Before we begin our review, remember that there is no wrong-answer penalty on this exam, so try not to leave an answer selection blank. Of course, since the objective is to get as many right answers as possible, always use the process of elimination before choosing your answer. While the amount of time allotted for this section may seem like too little for the amount of questions, many of the questions are designed to be simpler than others.

The Most Common Mistakes

People make mistakes all the time – but during a test, those mistakes can cost you a passing score. Watch out for these common mistakes that people make on the PARAPRO:

- Answering with the wrong sign (positive / negative).

- Mixing up the Order of Operations.

- Misplacing a decimal.

- Not reading the question thoroughly (and therefore providing an answer that was not asked for.)

- Circling the wrong letter, or filling in wrong circle choice.

If you're thinking, "Those ideas are just common sense" – exactly! Most of the mistakes made on the PARAPRO are simple mistakes. Regardless, they still result in a wrong answer and the loss of a potential point.

Helpful Strategies

- **Go Back to the Basics**: First and foremost, practice your basic skills: sign changes, order of operations, simplifying fractions, and equation manipulation. These are the skills used most on the test, though they are applied in different contexts. Remember that when it comes right down to it, all math problems rely on the four basic skills of addition, subtraction, multiplication, and division. All that changes is the order in which they are used to solve a problem.

- **Don't Rely on Mental Math**: Using mental math is great for eliminating answer choices, but ALWAYS WRITE IT DOWN! This cannot be stressed enough. Use whatever paper is provided; by writing and/or drawing out the problem, you are more likely to catch any mistakes. The act of writing things down forces you to organize your calculations, leading to an improvement in your score.

- **The Three-Times Rule**:

  1. **Step One – Read the question**: Write out the given information.

  2. **Step Two – Read the question**: Set up your equation(s) and solve.

  3. **Step Three – Read the question**: Make sure that your answer makes sense (is the amount too large or small, is the answer in the correct unit of measure, etc.).

- **Make an Educated Guess**: Eliminate those answer choices which you are relatively sure are incorrect, and then guess from the remaining choices. Educated guessing is critical to increasing your score.

Calculators

No calculators! It is very important that you do not let yourself cheat while practicing. You will only be cheating yourself out of a better score on test day.

Math Concepts Tested on the ParaPro

You need to practice in order to score well on the test. To make the most out of your practice, use this guide to determine the areas for which you need more review. Most importantly, practice all areas under testing circumstances (a quiet area, a timed practice test, no looking up facts as you practice, etc.)

When reviewing, take your time and let your brain recall the necessary math. If you are taking this test, then you have already had course instruction in these areas. The examples given will "jog" your memory.

The next few pages will cover various math subjects (starting with the basics, but in no particular order), along with worked examples.

Order of Operations

PEMDAS – Parentheses/Exponents/Multiply/Divide/Add/Subtract

Perform the operations within parentheses first, and then any exponents. After those steps, perform all multiplication and division as they appear in the problem, from left to right. Finally, do all required addition and subtraction as they appear in the problem.

Examples:

Solve (-(2)² - (4 + 7)).

(-4 – 11) = **– 15**.

Solve ((5)² ÷ 5 + 4 × 2).

25 ÷ 5 + 4 × 2.

5 + 8 = **13**.

Positive & Negative Number Rules

(+) + (−)	Subtract the two numbers. Solution keeps the sign of the larger number.
(−) + (−)	Negative number.
(+) × (−)	Negative number.
(−) × (−)	Positive number.
(+) ÷ (−)	Negative number.
(−) ÷ (−)	Positive number.

Fractions

A common denominator is required to add and subtract fractions.

Find a common denominator for:

$$\frac{2}{3} - \frac{1}{5}$$

$$\frac{2}{3} - \frac{1}{5} = \frac{2}{3}\left(\frac{5}{5}\right) - \frac{1}{5}\left(\frac{3}{3}\right) = \frac{10}{15} - \frac{3}{15} = \frac{7}{15}$$

To add mixed fractions, work first the whole numbers, and then the fractions.

$$2\frac{1}{4} + 1\frac{3}{4} = 3\frac{4}{4} = \mathbf{4}$$

To subtract mixed fractions, convert to single fractions by multiplying the whole number by the denominator and adding the numerator. Then work as above.

$$2\frac{1}{4} - 1\frac{3}{4} = \frac{9}{4} - \frac{7}{4} = \frac{2}{4} = \frac{1}{2}$$

To multiply fractions, convert any mixed fractions into single fractions and multiply across; reduce to lowest terms if needed.

$$2\frac{1}{4} \times 1\frac{3}{4} = \frac{9}{4} \times \frac{7}{4} = \frac{63}{16} = \mathbf{3\frac{15}{16}}$$

To divide fractions, convert any mixed fractions into single fractions, flip the second fraction, and then multiply across.

$$2\frac{1}{4} \div 1\frac{3}{4} = \frac{9}{4} \div \frac{7}{4} = \frac{9}{4} \times \frac{4}{7} = \frac{36}{28} = 1\frac{8}{28} = \mathbf{1\frac{2}{7}}$$

Absolute Value

A number's absolute value is its distance from zero, not its value.

So in $|x| = a$, "x" will equal "$-a$" as well as "a."

Likewise, $|\,3\,| = 3$, and $|-3\,| = 3$.

Equations with absolute values will have two answers. Solve each absolute value possibility separately. All solutions must be checked into the original equation.

Example: Solve for x:
$|2x - 3| = x + 1$.

Equation One: $2x - 3 = -(x + 1)$.
$\quad\quad\quad\quad\quad 2x - 3 = -x - 1$.
$\quad\quad\quad\quad\quad 3x = 2$.
$\quad\quad\quad\quad\quad \mathbf{x = 2/3}$.

Equation Two: $2x - 3 = x + 1$.
$\quad\quad\quad\quad\quad \mathbf{x = 4}$.

Simple Interest

Interest * Principle

Example: If I deposit $500 into an account with an annual rate of 5%, how much will I have after 2 years?

1st year: $500 + (500 \times .05) = 525$.

2nd year: $525 + (525 \times .05) = \mathbf{551.25}$.

Greatest Common Factor (GCF)

The greatest factor that divides two numbers.

Example: The GCF of 24 and 18 is 6. 6 is the largest number, or greatest factor, that can divide both 24 and 18.

Mean, Median, Mode

Mean is a math term for "average." Total all terms and divide by the number of terms.

Find the mean of 24, 27, and 18.

$24 + 27 + 18 = 69 \div 3 = $ **23**.

Median is the middle number of a given set, found after the numbers have all been put in numerical order. In the case of a set of even numbers, the middle two numbers are averaged.

What is the median of 24, 27, and 18?

18, **24**, 27.

What is the median of 24, 27, 18, and 19?

18, 19, 24, 27 (19 + 24 = 43. 43/2 = **21.5**).

Mode is the number which occurs most frequently within a given set.

What is the mode of 2, 5, 4, 4, 3, 2, 8, 9, 2, 7, 2, and 2?

The mode would be **2** because it appears the most within the set.

Percent, Part, & Whole

Part = Percent * Whole.

Percent = Part / Whole.

Whole = Part / Percent.

Example: Jim spent 30% of his paycheck at the fair. He spent $15 for a hat, $30 for a shirt, and $20 playing games. How much was his check? (Round to nearest dollar)

Whole = 65 / .30 = **$217.00**.

Percent Change

Percent Change = Amount of Change / Original Amount × 100.

Percent Increase = (New Amount – Original Amount) / Original Amount × 100.

Percent Decrease = (Original Amount – New Amount) / Original Amount × 100.

Amount Increase (or **Decrease**) = Original Price × Percent Markup (or Markdown).

Original Price = New Price / (Whole – Percent Markdown).

Original Price = New Price / (Whole + Percent Markup).

> **Example:** A car that was originally priced at $8300 has been reduced to $6995. What percent has it been reduced?
>
> (8300 – 6995) / 8300 × 100 = **15.72%**.

Repeated Percent Change

Increase: Final amount = Original Amount × $(1 + \text{Rate})^{\text{\# of changes}}$.

Decrease: Final Amount = Original Amount × $(1 - \text{Rate})^{\text{\# of changes}}$.

> **Example:** The weight of a tube of toothpaste decreases by 3% each time it is used. If it weighed 76.5 grams when new, what is its weight in grams after 15 uses?
>
> Final amount = $76.5 \times (1 - .3)^{15}$.
>
> $76.5 \times (.97)^{15}$ = **48.44 grams**.

Ratios

To solve a ratio, simply find the equivalent fraction. To distribute a whole across a ratio:

1. Total all parts.

2. Divide the whole by the total number of parts.

3. Multiply quotient by corresponding part of ratio.

Example: There are 90 voters in a room, and they are either Democrat or Republican. The ratio of Democrats to Republicans is 5:4. How many Republicans are there?

Step 1 $5 + 4 = 9$.

Step 2 $90 / 9 = 10$.

Step 3 $10 \times 4 = $ **40 Republicans**.

Proportions

Direct Proportions: Corresponding ratio parts change in the same direction (increase/decrease).

Indirect Proportions: Corresponding ratio parts change in opposite directions (as one part increases the other decreases).

Example: A train traveling 120 miles takes 3 hours to get to its destination. How long will it take if the train travels 180 miles?

120 mph:180 mph is to x hours:3 hours.

(Write as fraction and cross multiply.)

$120/3 = 180/x$.

$540 = 120x$.

$x = $ **4.5 hours**.

Probabilities

A probability is found by dividing the number of desired outcomes by the number of possible outcomes. (The piece divided by the whole.)

Example: What is the probability of picking a blue marble if 3 of the 15 marbles are blue?

$3/15 = 1/5$. The probability is **1 in 5** that a blue marble is picked.

Math and Quantitative Reasoning Sequence

Each term is equal to the previous term plus x.

Example: 2, 5, 8, 11.

$x = 3$.

$2 + 3 = 5; 5 + 3 = 8 \dots$ etc.

Geometric Sequence

Each term is equal to the previous term multiplied by x.

Example: 2, 4, 8, 16.

$x = 2$.

Prime Factorization

Expand to prime number factors.

Example: $104 = 2 * 2 * 2 * 13$.

Exponent Rules

Rule	Example
$x^0 = 1$	$5^0 = 1$
$x^1 = x$	$5^1 = 5$
$x^a \cdot x^b = x^{a+b}$	$5^2 \times 5^3 = 5^5$
$(xy)^a = x^a y^a$	$(5 \times 6)^2 = 5^2 \times 6^2 = 25 \times 36$
$(x^a)^b = x^{ab}$	$(5^2)^3 = 5^6$
$(x/y)^a = x^a/y^a$	$(10/5)^2 = 10^2/5^2 = 100/25$
$x^a/y^b = x^{a-b}$	$5^4/5^3 = 5^1 = 5$ (remember $x \neq 0$)
$x^{1/a} = \sqrt[a]{x}$	$25^{1/2} = \sqrt[2]{25} = 5$
$x^{-a} = \dfrac{1}{x^a}$	$5^{-2} = \dfrac{1}{5^2} = \dfrac{1}{25}$ (remember $x \neq 0$)
$(- x)^a$ = positive number if "a" is even; negative number if "a" is odd.	

Roots

Root of a Product: $\sqrt[n]{a \cdot b} = \sqrt[n]{a} \cdot \sqrt[n]{b}$

Root of a Quotient: $\sqrt[n]{\dfrac{a}{b}} = \dfrac{\sqrt[n]{a}}{\sqrt[n]{b}}$

Fractional Exponent: $\sqrt[n]{a^m} = a^{m/n}$

Literal Equations

Equations with more than one variable. Solve in terms of one variable first.

Example: Solve for y: $4x + 3y = 3x + 2y$.

Step 1 – Combine like terms: $3y - 2y = 4x - 2x$.

Step 2 – Solve for y: $y = 2x$.

Slope

The formula used to calculate the slope (m) of a straight line connecting two points is: $m = (y_2 - y_1) / (x_2 - x_1) = $ change in y / change in x.

Example: Calculate slope of the line in the diagram:

$m = (3 - (-1))/(-4 - 2) = 4/-6 = -2/3$.

Midpoint

To determine the midpoint between two points, simply add the two x coordinates together and divide by 2 (midpoint x). Then add the y coordinates together and divide by 2 (midpoint y).

$$\left(\frac{x_1 + x_2}{2}, \frac{y_1 + y}{2} \right)$$

Algebraic Equations

When simplifying or solving algebraic equations, you need to be able to utilize all math rules: exponents, roots, negatives, order of operations, etc.

1. Add & Subtract: Only the coefficients of like terms.

   Example: $5xy + 7y + 2yz + 11xy - 5yz = 16xy + 7y - 3yz$.

2. Multiplication: First the coefficients then the variables.

   Example: Monomial × Monomial.

   $(3x^4y^2z)(2y^4z^5) = 6x^4y^6z^6$.

   (A variable with no exponent has an implied exponent of 1.)

   Example: Monomial × Polynomial.

   $(2y^2)(y^3 + 2xy^2z + 4z) = 2y^5 + 4xy^4z + 8y^2z$.

71

Example: Binomial × Binomial.

$(5x + 2)(3x + 3)$.

(Remember FOIL – First, Outer, Inner, Last.)

First: $5x \times 3x = 15x^2$.

Outer: $5x \times 3 = 15x$.

Inner: $2 \times 3x = 6x$.

Last: $2 \times 3 = 6$.

Combine like terms: $15x^2 + 21x + 6$.

Example: Binomial × Polynomial.

$(x + 3)(2x^2 - 5x - 2)$.

First term: $x(2x^2 - 5x - 2) = 2x^3 - 5x^2 - 2x$.

Second term: $3(2x^2 - 5x - 2) = 6x^2 - 15x - 6$.

Added Together: $2x^3 + x^2 - 17x - 6$.

Inequalities

Inequalities are solved like linear and algebraic equations, except the sign must be reversed when dividing by a negative number.

Example: $-7x + 2 < 6 - 5x$.

Step 1 – Combine like terms: $-2x < 4$.

Step 2 – Solve for x. (Reverse the sign): **$x > $ -2.**

Solving compound inequalities will give you two answers.

Example: $-4 \leq 2x - 2 \leq 6$.

Step 1 – Add 2 to each term to isolate x: $-2 \leq 2x \leq 8$.

Step 2: Divide by 2: $-1 \leq x \leq 4$.

Solution set is **[-1, 4]**.

Fundamental Counting Principle

(The number of possibilities of an event happening) * (the number of possibilities of another event happening) = the total number of possibilities.

Example: If you take a 5-question multiple choice test, in which each question has 4 answer choices, how many test result possibilities are there?

Solution: Question 1 has 4 choices; question 2 has 4 choices; etc.

$4 \times 4 \times 4 \times 4 \times 4$ (one for each question) = **1024 possible test results**.

Permutations

The number of ways a set number of items can be arranged. Recognized by the use of a factorial ($n!$), with n being the number of items.

If $n = 3$, then $3! = 3 \times 2 \times 1 = 6$. If you need to arrange n number of things but x number are alike, then n! is divided by $x!$

Example: How many different arrangements can be made of the letters in the word **balance**?

Solution: There are 7 letters so $n! = 7!$ and two letters are the same so $x! = 2!$ Set up the equation:

$$\frac{7 \times 6 \times 5 \times 4 \times 3 \times 2 \times 1}{2 \times 1} = \textbf{2540 ways}.$$

Combinations

To calculate total number of possible combinations use the formula:
n!/r! (n-r)!   n = # of objects   r = # of objects selected at a time

Example: If seven people are selected in groups of three, how many different combinations are possible?

Solution:
$$\frac{7 \times 6 \times 5 \times 4 \times 3 \times 2 \times 1}{(3 \times 2 \times 1)(7 - 3)} = \textbf{210 possible combinations}.$$

Geometry

- **Obtuse Angle**: Measures greater than 90º.

- **Obtuse Triangle**: One angle measures greater than 90º.

- Acute Angle: Measures less than 90º.

- **Acute Triangle**: Each angle measures less than 90º.

- **Adjacent Angles**: Share a side and a vertex.

- **Complementary Angles**: Adjacent angles that sum to 90º.

- **Supplementary Angles**: Adjacent angles that sum to 180º.

- **Vertical Angles**: Angles that are opposite of each other. They are always congruent (equal in measure).

- **Isosceles Triangle**: Two sides and two angles are equivalent.

- **Equilateral Triangle**: All angles are equivalent.

- **Scalene**: No equal angles.

- **Parallel Lines**: Lines that will never intersect. Y **ll** X means line Y is parallel to line X.

- **Perpendicular lines**: Lines that cross, forming 90º angles.

- **Transversal Line**: A line that crosses parallel lines.

- **Bisector**: Any line that cuts a line segment, angle, or polygon exactly in half.

- **Polygon**: Any enclosed plane shape comprised of three or more connecting sides (ex. a triangle).

- **Regular Polygon**: Has all equal sides and equal angles (ex. square).

- **Arc**: A portion of a circle's edge.

- **Chord**: A line segment that connects two different points on a circle.

- **Tangent**: Something that touches a circle at only one point without crossing through it.

- **Sum of Angles**: The sum of a polygon's angles can be calculated using $(n-1)180º$, when n = the number of sides

Regular Polygons

Polygon Angle Principle: S = The sum of interior angles of a polygon with n-sides.

$S = (n - 2)180.$

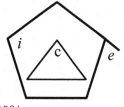

The measure of each central angle (c) is $360°/n$.
The measure of each interior angle (i) is $(n - 2)180°/n$.
The measure of each exterior angle (e) is $360°/n$.

To compare areas of similar polygons: $A_1/A_2 = (side_1/side_2)^2$.

Triangles

The angles in a triangle add up to $180°$.

Area of a triangle = $\frac{1}{2} * b * h$, or $\frac{1}{2}bh$.

Pythagoras' Theorem: $a^2 + b^2 = c^2$

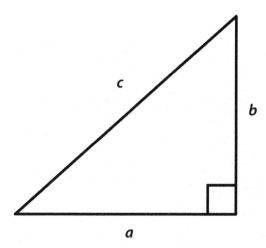

Trapezoids

Four-sided polygon, in which the bases (and only the bases) are parallel.
Isosceles Trapezoid – base angles are congruent.

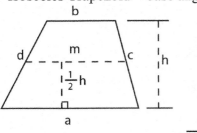

Area and Perimeter of a Trapezoid

$$m = \frac{1}{2}(a+b)$$

$$Area = \frac{1}{2}h*(a+b) = m*h$$

$$Perimeter = a+b+c+d = 2m+c+d$$

If m is the median then: $m \parallel \overline{AB}$ and $m \parallel \overline{CD}$

Rhombus

Four-sided polygon, in which opposite sides are parallel and all four sides are congruent.

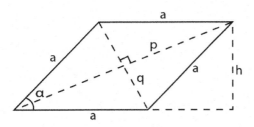

Area and Perimeter of a Rhombus

$$Perimeter = 4a$$

$$Area = a^2 \sin\alpha = a*h = \frac{1}{2}pq$$

$$4a^2 = p^2 + q^2$$

Rectangle

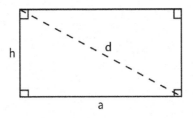

Area and Perimeter of a Rectangle

$$d = \sqrt{a^2 + h^2}$$

$$a = \sqrt{d^2 - h^2}$$

$$h = \sqrt{d^2 - a^2}$$

$$Perimeter = 2a + 2h$$

$$Area = a \cdot h$$

Square

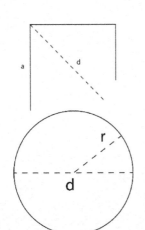

Area and Perimeter of a Square

$$d = a\sqrt{2}$$

$$Perimeter = 4a = 2d\sqrt{2}$$

$$Area = a^2 = \frac{1}{2}d^2$$

Circle

Area and Perimeter of a Circle

$$d = 2r$$

$$Perimeter = 2\pi r = \pi d$$

76 $Area = \pi r^2$

Cube

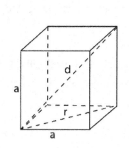

Area and Volume of a Cube

$r = a\sqrt{2}$

$d = a\sqrt{3}$

$Area = 6a^2$

$Volume = a^3$

Cuboid

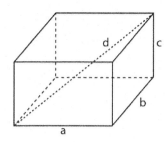

Area and Volume of a Cuboid

$d = \sqrt{a^2 + b^2 + c^2}$

$A = 2(ab + ac + bc)$

$V = abc$

Pyramid

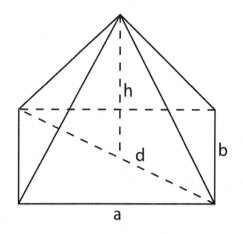

Area and Volume of a Pyramid

$A_{lateral} = a\sqrt{h^2 + \left(\frac{b}{2}\right)^2} + b\sqrt{h^2 + \left(\frac{a}{2}\right)^2}$

$d = \sqrt{a^2 + b^2}$

$A_{base} = ab$

$A_{total} = A_{lateral} + A_{base}$

$V = \frac{1}{3}abh$

The following pages will provide a series of tests for the different subjects and sections which you may encounter on the exam. Please note that these questions will not necessarily appear in the same format as they will on the exam – rather, they are testing your fundamental knowledge and comprehension of their subjects. As you take these practice tests, mark those questions with which you have difficulty or have answered incorrectly. Make a note of them so that you know what to focus your studies on.

Most importantly: don't over-exert yourself. The following practice tests are rather extensive. Pace yourself – don't rush through them. This is a review, an assessment of your current level of comprehension. It's not a race. That said – best of luck!

The following pages will provide a series of tests for the different subjects and sections which you may encounter on the exam. Please note that these questions will not necessarily appear in the same format as they will on the exam – rather, they are testing your fundamental knowledge and comprehension of their subjects. As you take these practice tests, mark those questions with which you have difficulty or have answered incorrectly. Make a note of them so that you know what to focus your studies on.

Most importantly: don't over-exert yourself. The following practice tests are rather extensive. Pace yourself – don't rush through them. This is a review, an assessment of your current level of comprehension. It's not a race. That said – best of luck!

1. In a class of 42 students, 18 are boys. Two girls get transferred to another school. What percent of students remaining are girls?
    a) 14%.
    b) 16%.
    c) 52.4%.
    d) 60%.
    e) None of the above.

2. A payroll check is issued for $500.00. If 20% goes to bills, 30% of the remainder goes to pay entertainment expenses, and 10% of what is left is placed in a retirement account, then approximately how much is remaining?
    a) $150.
    b) $250.
    c) $170.
    d) $350.
    e) $180.

3. A painting by Van Gogh increased in value by 80% from year 1995 to year 2000. If in year 2000, the painting is worth $7200, what was its value in 1995?
    a) $1500.
    b) $2500.
    c) $3000.
    d) $4000.
    e) $5000.

4. "Dresses and Ties" sells a particular dress for $60 dollars. But, they decide to discount the price of that dress by 25%. How much does the dress cost now?
    a) $55.
    b) $43.
    c) $45.
    d) $48.
    e) $65.

5. A sweater goes on sale for 30% off. If the original price was $70, what is the discounted price?
    a) $48.
    b) $49.
    c) $51.
    d) $65.
    e) $52.

6. If the value of a car depreciates by 60% over ten years, and its value in the year 2000 is $2500, what was its value in the year 1990?
    a) $6000.
    b) $6230.
    c) $6250.
    d) $6500.
    e) $6600.

7. If an account is opened with a starting balance of $500, what is the amount in the account after 3 years if the account pays compound interest of 5%?
    a) $560.80.
    b) $578.81.
    c) $564.50.
    d) $655.10.
    e) $660.00.

8. A piece of memorabilia depreciates by 1% every year. If the value of the memorabilia is $75000, what will it be 2 years from now? Give the answer as a whole number.
    a) $74149.
    b) $74150.
    c) $73151.
    d) $71662.
    e) $73507.

9. A dress is marked down by 20% in an effort to boost sales for one week. After that week, the price of the dress is brought back to the original value. What percent did the price of the dress have to be increased from its discounted price?
    a) 20%.
    b) 25%.
    c) 120%.
    d) 125%.
    e) 15%.

10. A car dealer increases the price of a car by 30%, but then discounts it by 30%. What is the relationship between the final price and the original price?
    a) $.91x : x$.
    b) $.98x : x$.
    c) 1:1.
    d) $.88x : x$.
    e) $.75x : x$.

1. **e)**

   The entire class has 42 students, 18 of which are boys, meaning 42 - 18 = 24 is the number of girls. Out of these 24 girls, 2 leave; so 22 girls are left. The total number of students is now 42 - 2 = 40.

   22/40 * 100 = 55%.

   Reminder: If you forget to subtract 2 from the total number of students, you will end up with 60% as the answer. Sometimes you may calculate an answer that has been given as a choice; it can still be incorrect. Always check your answer.

2. **b)**

   If out of the entire paycheck, 20% is first taken out, then the remainder is 80%. Of this remainder, if 30% is used for entertainment, then (.8 - .80 * .30) = .560 is left. If 10% is put into a retirement account, then (.56 - .56 * .1) = .504 is remaining. So out of $500, the part that remains is 50%, which is $252.

3. **d)**

   In 2005, the value was 1.8 times its value in 1995. So $1.8x = 7200 \rightarrow x = 4000$.

4. **c)**

   60 * (100 - 25)/100 $\rightarrow$ 60 * .75 = 45.

5. **b)**

   New price = original price * (1 – discount) $\rightarrow$ new price = 70(1-.3) = 49.

6. **c)**

   $Value_{2000}$ = Original price * (1-.6) $\rightarrow$ 2500 = .4P = 2500 $\rightarrow$ P = 6250.

7. **b)**

   Amount = $P(1 + r)^t$ = 500 * 1.05^3 = $578.81.

8. **e)**

   Final value = $75000(1 - .1)^2$ = 73507.

9. **b)**

   If the original price of the dress was x, then the discounted price would be $0.8x$. To increase the price from $.8x$ to x, the percent increase would be $(x - .8x)/.8x * 100 = 25\%$.

10. **a)**

    Let the original price of the car be x. After the 30% increase, the price is $1.3x$.

    After discounting the increased price by 30%, it now is $.7 * 1.3x = .91x$.

    Therefore, the ratio of the final price to the original price = $.91x : x$.

1. If test A is taken 5 times with an average result of 21, and test B is taken 13 times with an average result of 23, what is the combined average?
    a) 22.24.
    b) 22.22.
    c) 22.00.
    d) 22.44.
    e) 24.22.

2. A set of data has 12 entries. The average of the first 6 entries is 12, the average of the next two entries is 20, and the average of the remaining entries is 4. What is the average of the entire data set?
    a) 10.
    b) 10.67.
    c) 11.
    d) 12.67.
    e) 10.5.

3. What is the average score of 8 tests where the score for 3 tests is 55, the score for two tests is 35, and the remaining tests have scores of 70?
    a) 50.3.
    b) 52.5.
    c) 55.1.
    d) 56.0.
    e) 55.6.

4. The temperatures over a week are recorded as follows:

Day	High	Low
Monday	80	45
Tuesday	95	34
Wednesday	78	47
Thursday	79	55
Friday	94	35
Saturday	67	46
Sunday	76	54

What is the approximate average high temperature and average low temperature during the week?
    a) 90, 50.
    b) 80, 40.
    c) 81, 45.
    d) 82, 46.
    e) 81, 47.

5. Twelve teams competed in a mathematics test. The scores recorded for each team are: 29, 30, 28, 27, 35, 43, 45, 50, 46, 37, 44, and 41. What is the median score?

   a) 37.
   b) 41.
   c) 39.
   d) 44.
   e) 45.

1. d)

If test A avg = 21 for 5 tests, then sum of test A results = 21 * 5 = 105.
If test B avg = 23 for 13 tests, then sum of test B results = 23 * 13 = 299.
So total result = 299 + 105 = 404.
Average of all tests = 404/(5 + 13) = 404/18 = 22.44.

2. b)

The average of the first 6 points is 12 → $s_1/6 = 12$ → $s_1 = 72$; s_1 is the sum of the first 6 points.

The average of the next 2 points is 20 → $s_2/2 = 20$ → $s_2 = 40$; s_2 is the sum of the next 2 points.

The average of the remaining 4 points is 4 → $s_3/4 = 4$ → $s_3 = 16$; s_3 is the sum of the last 4 points.

The sum of all the data points = 72 + 40 + 16 = 128.

The average = 128/12 = 10.67.

3. e)

Average = (3 * 55 + 2 * 35 + 3 * 70)/8 → Average = 55.625.

4. c)

Average of high s = (80 + 95 + 78 + 79 + 94 + 67 + 76)/7 = 81.29.

Average of low s = (45 + 34 + 47 + 55 + 35 + 46 + 54)/7 = 45.14.

5. c)

To find the median, we first have to put the list in order:

27, 28, 29, 30, 35, 37, 41, 43, 44, 45, 46, 50.

The middle two scores are 37 and 41, and their average is 39.

e) None of the above

The mean is just the total score/number of scores → 90 +... + 94)/10 → 79.9.

The median is the score located in the middle. The middle of the set of the numbers is between 84 and 79. The average of these two scores is 81.5.

The mode is the number that occurs the most: 78.

1. What is $x^2y^3z^5/y^2z^{-9}$?
   a) y^5z^4.
   b) yz^4.
   c) x^2yz^{14}.
   d) $x^2y^5z^4$.
   e) xyz.

2. What is k if $(2m^3)^5 = 32m^{k+1}$?
   a) 11.
   b) 12.
   c) 13.
   d) 14.
   e) 15.

3. What is $x^5y^4z^3/x^{-3}y^2z^{-4}$?
   a) $x^6y^4z^7$.
   b) x^8yz^7.
   c) x^6yz^7.
   d) $x^8y^2z^7$.
   e) $x^6y^2z^7$.

4. Evaluate $(a^2 * a^{54} + a^{56} + (a^{58}/a^2))/a^4$.
   a) a^{56}.
   b) $3a^{56}$.
   c) $3a^{52}$.
   d) $3a^{54}$.
   e) a^{54}.

5. $9^m = 3^{-1/n}$. What is mn?
   a) .5.
   b) 2.
   c) -2.
   d) -.5.
   e) -1.

6. If $2^a * 4^a = 32$, what is a?
   a) 1/3.
   b) 2/3.
   c) 1.
   d) 4/3.
   e) 5/3.

1. **c)**
   $x^2y^3z^5/y^2z^{-9} = x^2y^3z^5 * y^{-2}z^9$ which gives the answer $x^2y^{(3-2)}z^{(5+9)}$ → x^2yz^{14}.

2. **d)**
   Expand $(2m^3)^5$ to give $32m^{15}$.

   So $32m^{15} = 32m^{k+1}$ → $k+1 = 15$ → $k = 14$.

3. **d)**
   $x^5y^4z^3/x^{-3}y^2z^{-4} = x^5y^4z^3 * x^3y^{-2}z^4 = x^8y^2z^7$.

4. **c)**
   $(a^2*a^{54}+a^{56}+ (a^{58}/a^2))/a^4 = (a^{54+2}+a^{56}+a^{58-2})a^{-4} = 3a^{56-4} = 3a^{52}$.

5. **d)**
   9^m is the same as 3^{2m}.

   So $3^{2m} = 3^{-1/n}$ → $2m = -1/n$ → $mn = -.5$.

6. **e)**
   $2^a * 4^a$ can be re-written as $2^a * (2^2)^a$.

   $32 = 2^5$.

   Therefore, $2^{(a+2a)} = 2^5$ → $3a = 5$ → $a = 5/3$.

1. The number $568cd$ should be divisible by 2, 5, and 7. What are the values of the digits c and d?
   a) 56835.
   b) 56830.
   c) 56860.
   d) 56840.
   e) 56800.

2. Carla is 3 times older than her sister Megan. Eight years ago, Carla was 18 years older than her sister. What is Megan's age?
   a) 10.
   b) 8.
   c) 9.
   d) 6.
   e) 5.

3. What is the value of $f(x) = (x^2 - 25)/(x + 5)$ when $x = 0$?
   a) -1.
   b) -2.
   c) -3.
   d) -4.
   e) -5.

4. Four years from now, John will be twice as old as Sally will be. If Sally was 10 eight years ago, how old is John?
   a) 35.
   b) 40.
   c) 45.
   d) 50.
   e) 55.

5. I have some marbles. I give 25% to Vic, 20% to Robbie, 10% to Jules. I then give 6/20 of the remaining amount to my brother, and keep the rest for myself. If I end up with 315 marbles, how many did I have to begin with?
   a) 1000.
   b) 1500.
   c) 3500.
   d) 400.
   e) 500.

6. I have some marbles. I give 25% to Vic, 20% of the remainder to Robbie, 10% of that remainder to Jules and myself I then give 6/20 of the remaining amount to my brother, and keep the rest for myself. If I end up with 315 marbles, how many did I have to begin with?
   a) 800.
   b) 833.
   c) 834.
   d) 378.
   e) 500.

7. If $x = 5y + 4$, what is the value of y if $x = 29$?

    a) 33/5.

    b) 5.5.

    c) 5.

    d) 0.

    e) 29/5.

8. A bag of marbles has 8 marbles. If I buy 2 bags of marbles, how many more bags of marbles would I need to buy to have a total of at least 45 marbles?

    a) 3.

    b) 4.

    c) 5.

    d) 6.

    e) 29.

9. A factory that produces widgets wants to sell them each for $550. It costs $50 for the raw materials for each widget, and the startup cost for the factory was $10000. How many widgets have to be sold so that the factory can break even?

    a) 10.

    b) 20.

    c) 30.

    d) 40.

    e) 50.

10. Expand $(3x - 4)(6 - 2x)$.

    a) $6x^2 - 6x + 8$.

    b) $-6x^2 + 26x - 24$.

    c) $6x^2 - 26x + 24$.

    d) $-6x^2 + 26x + 24$.

    e) $6x^2 + 26x - 24$.

11. If $6n + m$ is divisible by 3 and 5, which of the following numbers when added to $6n + m$ will still give a result that is divisible by 3 and 5?

    a) 4.

    b) 6.

    c) 12.

    d) 20.

    e) 60.

12. If x is negative, and $x^3/5$ and $x/5$ both give the same result, what could be the value of x?

    a) -5.

    b) -4.

    c) 3.

    d) 0.

    e) -1.

13. If $m = 3548$, and $n = 235$, then what is the value of $m * n$?
- a) 87940.
- b) 843499.
- c) 87900.
- d) 8830.
- e) 833780.

14. A ball is thrown at a speed of 30 mph. How far will it travel in 2 minutes and 35 seconds?
- a) 1.5 miles.
- b) 1.20 miles.
- c) 1.29 miles.
- d) 1.3 miles.
- e) 1.1 miles.

15. Simplify: $30(\sqrt{40} - \sqrt{60})$.
- a) $30(\sqrt{5} - \sqrt{15})$.
- b) $30(\sqrt{10} + \sqrt{15})$.
- c) $60(\sqrt{5} + \sqrt{15})$.
- d) $60(\sqrt{10} - \sqrt{15})$.
- e) 60.

16. Simplify: $30/(\sqrt{40} - \sqrt{60})$.
- a) $3(\sqrt{5} + \sqrt{15})$.
- b) $-3(\sqrt{5} - \sqrt{15})$.
- c) $-3(\sqrt{10} + \sqrt{15})$.
- d) $3(\sqrt{10} + \sqrt{15})$.
- e) $3(\sqrt{10} - \sqrt{15})$.

17. What is the least common multiple of 2, 3, 4, and 5?
- a) 30.
- b) 60.
- c) 120.
- d) 40.
- e) 50.

18. It costs $6 to make a pen that sells for $12. How many pens need to be sold to make a profit of $60?
- a) 10.
- b) 6.
- c) 72.
- d) 30.
- e) 12.

1. **d)**

   If the number is divisible by 2, d should be even. If the number is divisible by 5, then b has to equal 0.

   Start by making both variables 0 and dividing by the largest factor, 7.

   $56800/7 = 8114$.

   2 from 56800 is 56798, a number divisible by 2 and 7.

   Next add a multiple of 7 that turns the last number to a 0. $6 * 7 = 42$. $56798 + 42 = 56840$, which is divisible by 2, 5, and 7.

2. **c)**

   Carla's age is c; Megan's age is m. $c = 3m$; $c - 8 = m - 8 + 18$.

   Substitute $3m$ for c in equation 2 → $3m - 8 = m + 10$ → $m = 9$.

3. **e)**

   We know $(x^2 - 25) = (x + 5)(x - 5)$.

   So $(x^2 - 25)/(x + 5) = x - 5$. At $x = 0$, $f(0) = -5$.

4. **b)**

   Let j be John's age and s be Sally's age.

   $j + 4 = 2(s + 4)$.

   $s - 8 = 10$ → $s = 18$.

   So $j + 4 = 2(18 + 4)$ → $j = 40$.

5. **a)**

   If x is the number of marbles initially, then $.25x$ goes to Vic, $.2x$ goes to Robbie, and $.1x$ goes to Jules.

   The number left, x, is $(1 - .25 - .2 - .1) = .45x$.

   Of that I give 6/20 to my brother, so $6/20 * .45x$.

   I am left with $.45x(1 - (6/20)) = .315x$.

   We are also told $.315x = 315$ → $x = 1000$.

6. c)

Always read the question carefully! Questions 5 and 6 are similar, but they are not the same.

Let x be the original number of marbles. After Vic's share is given $.75x$ remains. After Robbie's share $.75x * .80$ remains. After Jules' share, $.75x * .8 * .9$ remains.

After I give my brother his share, $.75x * .8 * .9 * (1 - 6/20)$ remains. The remaining number $= .378x$.

We are told $.378x = 315 \rightarrow x = 833.33$. We need to increase this to the next highest number, 834, because we have part of a marble and to include it we need to have a whole marble.

7. c)

Replace the value of x with its value and solve the equation.

$29 = 5y + 4$.

Solving:

$29 - 4 = 5y + 4 - 4$.

$25 = 5y$ or $5y = 25$.

$5y/5 = 25/5$.

$y = 5$.

8. b)

$2(8) + x > 45$ means $x > 29$, so we need more than 29 marbles. A bag has 8 marbles, so the number of bags needed is 29/8, or 3.625. Since we need 3 bags + part of another bag, we need 4 additional bags to give at least 45 marbles.

9. b)

n is the number of widgets. The cost the factory incurs for making n widgets is $10000 + 50n$. The amount the factory makes by selling n widgets is $550n$.

At the break-even point, the cost incurred is equal to the amount of sales.

$10000 + 50n = 550n \rightarrow n = 20$.

10. b)

Use FOIL:

$(3x - 4)(6 - 2x) = 3x * 6 - 4 * 6 + 3x * (-2x) - 4 * (-2x) = 18x - 24 - 6x^2 + 8x = -6x^2 + 26x - 24$.

11. e)

Since $6n + m$ is divisible by 3 and 5, the new number that we get after adding a value will be divisible by 3 and 5 only if the value that we add is divisible by 3 and 5. The only number that will work from the given choices is 60.

12. e)

We are told $x^3/5 = x/5 \rightarrow x^3 = x$. The possible values are -1, 0, and 1. We are told that x is negative.

So $x = -1$.

13. e)

This problem can be done by elimination. We know that m is in the thousands, which means $x * 10^3$; and n is in the hundreds, which is $y * 10^2$. The answer will be $z * 10^5$, or 6 places in total, so we can eliminate **a)**, **c)**, and **d)**. Also we see that m ends in 8 and n ends in 5, so the answer has to end in 0 ($8 * 5 = 40$), which eliminates **b)**.

14. c)

The ball has a speed of 30 miles per hour. 30 miles per 60 minutes = .5 mile per minute; 2 minutes and 35 seconds = 2 minutes; and 35/60 minutes = 2.58 minutes.

The ball travels $.5 * 2.58 = 1.29$ miles.

15. d)

$$30\left(\sqrt{40} - \sqrt{60}\right) = 30\sqrt{4\,(10 - 15)} = 60\left(\sqrt{10} - \sqrt{15}\right).$$

16. c)

Multiply the numerator and the denominator by $\left(\sqrt{40} + \sqrt{60}\right)$.

So $30/\left(\sqrt{40} - \sqrt{60}\right) * \left[\left(\sqrt{40} + \sqrt{60}\right)/\left(\sqrt{40} + \sqrt{60}\right)\right] = 30\left(\sqrt{40} + \sqrt{60}\right)/\left(\sqrt{40} - \sqrt{60}\right)^2.$

$-3\left(\sqrt{10} + \sqrt{15}\right).$

17. b)

Find all the prime numbers that multiply to give the numbers.

For 2, prime factor is 2; for 3, prime factor is 3; for 4, prime factors are 2, 2; and for 5, prime factor is 5. Note the maximum times of occurrence of each prime and multiply these to find the least common multiple.

The LCM is $2 * 2 * 3 * 5 = 60$.

18. a)

One pen sells for $12, so on the sale of a pen, the profit is $12 - 6 = 6$.

In order to make $60, we need to sell 10 pens.

1. If $x < 5$ and $y < 6$, then $x + y$ __?__ 11.
   a) $<$
   b) $>$
   c) $\leq$
   d) $\geq$
   e) $=$

2. Which of the following is true about the inequality $25x^2 - 40x - 32 < 22$?
   a) There are no solutions.
   b) There is a set of solutions.
   c) There is 1 solution only.
   d) There are 2 solutions.
   e) There are 3 solutions.

3. If $x - 2y > 6$, what possible values of y always have x as greater than or equal to 2?
   a) $y \geq 1$.
   b) $y \leq 0$.
   c) $y \geq -2$.
   d) $y < 2$.
   e) $y \leq 6$.

4. Find the point of intersection of the lines $x + 2y = 4$ and $3x - y = 26$.
   a) $(1, 3)$.
   b) $(8, -2)$.
   c) $(0, 2)$.
   d) $(2, -1)$.
   e) $(4, 26)$.

5. If $a + b = 2$, and $a - b = 4$, what is a?
   a) 1.
   b) 2.
   c) 3.
   d) 4.
   e) 5.

6. If $\sqrt{a} + \sqrt{b} = 2$, and $\sqrt{a} - \sqrt{b} = 3$, what is $a + b$?
   a) 6.5.
   b) 6.
   c) 5.5.
   d) 5.
   e) 4.5.

7. If $a = b + 3$, and $3b = 5a + 6$, what is $3a - 2b$?
   a) -1.5.
   b) 2.5.
   c) 3.
   d) 4.3.
   e) 5.

8. The sum of the roots of a quadratic equation is 8, and the difference is 2. What is the equation?
   a) $x^2 - 8x - 15$.
   b) $x^2 + 8x + 15$.
   c) $x^2 - 8x + 15$.
   d) $x^2 + 8x - 15$.
   e) $x^2 + 15$.

9. Solve the following system of equations: $3x + 2y = 7$ and $3x + y = 5$.
   a) $x = 2, y = 1$.
   b) $x = 2, y = 2$.
   c) $x = 1, y = 0$.
   d) $x = 1, y = 2$.
   e) $x = 1, y = 1$.

10. Nine tickets were sold for $41. If the tickets cost $4 and $5, how many $5 tickets were sold?
    a) 5.
    b) 4.
    c) 9.
    d) 6.
    e) 7.

11. Joe brought a bag of 140 M&Ms to his class of 40 students. Each boy received 2 M&Ms. Each girl received 4. How many boys were in the class?
    a) 10.
    b) 20.
    c) 30.
    d) 40.
    e) 50.

1. **a)**
   Choice **a)** will always be true, while the other choices can never be true.

2. **b)**
   $25x^2 - 40x + 32 < 22$ → $25x^2 - 40x + 16 < 6$ → $(5x - 4)^2 < 6$ → $5x - 4 < 6$.

   $x = 2$, so x has to be all numbers less than 2 for this inequality to work.

3. **c)**
   Rearrange equation $x > 6 + 2y$, so $2 > 6 + 2y$. Solve for y.

   $2 \geq 6 + 2y$.

   $-4 \geq 2y$, so $-2 \leq y$ or $y \geq -2$.

   (When working with inequalities, remember to reverse the sign when dividing by a negative number.)

4. **b)**
   Find the slopes first. If they are not equal, then the lines intersect. The slopes are -1/2 and 3.

   Next, solve by substitution or addition. From the first equation, $x = 4 - 2y$. Plugging this into equation 2, we get $3(4 - 2y) - y = 26$ → $7y = 12 - 26$ → $y = -2$. Plug this value into either equation to find x.

   With equation 1, we get $x - 4 = 4$ → $x = 8$.

5. **c)**

   Add the equations to eliminate b. $2a = 6$ → $a = 3$.

6. **a)**
   Square both equations.

   Equation 1 becomes $a + 2\sqrt{ab} + b = 4$; and equation 2 becomes $a - 2\sqrt{ab} + b = 9$.

   Add the equations.
   $2(a + b) = 13$ → $a + b = 13/2$. $13/2 = 6.5$.

7. **a)**

Solve by substitution.

If $a = b + 3$, and $3b = 5a + 6$, then $3b = 5(b+3) + 6$.

If $3b - 5b - 15 = 6$, then $-2b = 21$. Therefore, $b = -10.5$.

Now use substitution to find a.

$a = b + 3$. So $a = -10.5 + 3$. Therefore, $a = -7.5$.

Solve the equation, $3a - 2b$.

$3(-7.5) - 2(-10.5) = -1.5$.

8. c)
If the roots are a and b, then $a + b = 8$ and $a - b = 2$.

Add the equations. $2a = 10 \rightarrow a = 5 \rightarrow b = 3$.

The factors are $(x - 5)(x - 3)$, and the equation is $x^2 - 8x + 15$.

9. d)
From the equation $3x + y = 5$, we get $y = 5 - 3x$. Substitute into the other equation. $3x + 2(5 - 3x) = 7$ $\rightarrow 3x + 10 - 6x = 7 \rightarrow x = 1$. This value into either of the equations gives us $y = 2$.

10. a)
$4x + 5y = 41$, and $x + y = 9$, where x and y are the number of tickets sold.

From equation 2: $x = 9 - y$.

From equation 1: $4(9 - y) + 5y = 41 \rightarrow 36 + y = 41 \rightarrow y = 5$.

11. a)
b is the number of boys, and g is the number of girls. So $b + g = 40$, and $2b + 4g = 140$.

To do the problem, use the substitution method. Plug ($g = 40 - b$) into ($2b + 4g = 140$).

$2b + 4(40 - b) = 140 \rightarrow b = 10$.

1. What is the equation of the line that passes through (3, 5), with intercept $y = 8$?
    a) $y = x + 8$.
    b) $y = x - 8$.
    c) $y = -x - 8$.
    d) $y = -x + 8$.
    e) $y = -x$.

2. What is the value of y in the equation $(3x - 4)^2 = 4y - 15$, if $x = 3$?
    a) 10.
    b) 2.5.
    c) -10.
    d) -2.5.
    e) 5.

3. If $y = 4x + 6y$, what is the range of y if $-10 < x \leq 5$?
    a) $-4 < y \leq 8$.
    b) $-4 < y < 8$.
    c) $8 > y > -4$.
    d) $-4 \leq y < 8$.
    e) $-4 \leq y \leq 8$.

4. If Jennifer gets three times as much allowance as Judy gets, and Judy gets $5/week, how much does Jennifer get every month?
    a) $15.
    b) $20.
    c) $30.
    d) $45.
    e) $60.

5. What is the value of x, if $y = 8$ in the equation $5x + 9y = 3x - 6y + 5$?
    a) 57.5.
    b) 60.
    c) -60.
    d) -57.5.
    e) None of the above.

6. What is the area outside the circle, but within the square whose two corners are A and B?

A (3, 5)   B (8, 17)

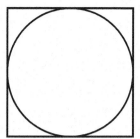

  a) 169(1-π).
  b) 169 π.
  c) 169 π /4.
  d) 169(1- π /4).
  e) 169.

7. Determine where the following two lines intersect:
$$3x + 4y = 7$$
$$9x + 12y = 21$$

  a) $x = 4, y = 3$.
  b) $x = 12, y = 9$.
  c) $x = 1/3, y = 1/3$.
  d) Not enough information provided.
  e) There is no solution; the lines do not intersect.

8. A line with a slope of 2 passes through the point (2, 4). What is the set of coordinates where that line passes through the y intercept?
  a) (-2, 0).
  b) (0, 0).
  c) (2, 2).
  d) (4, 0).
  e) (1, 1).

9. Are the following lines parallel or perpendicular?
$$3x + 4y = 7$$
$$8x - 6y = 9$$

  a) Parallel.
  b) Perpendicular.
  c) Neither parallel nor perpendicular.
  d) Cannot be determined.
  e) The angle at the point of intersection is 40.

10. Is the graph of the function $f(x) = -3x^2 + 4$ linear, asymptotical, symmetrical to the x axis, symmetrical to the y axis, or not symmetrical to either axis?

    a) Symmetrical to the x axis.
    b) Symmetrical to the y axis.
    c) Symmetrical to neither axis.
    d) Asymptotic.
    e) Linear.

11. Two points on a line have coordinates (3, 12) and (9, 20). What is the distance between these two points?

    a) 10.
    b) 12.
    c) 13.
    d) 8.
    e) 11.

13. What is the equation of a line passing through (1, 2) and (6, 12)?

    a) $y = x$.
    b) $y = 2x$.
    c) $y = x/2$.
    d) $y = 2x + 2$.
    e) $y = x - 2$.

14. What is the midpoint of the line connecting points (0, 8) and (2, 6)?

    a) (-1, 1).
    b) (2, 14).
    c) (-2, 2).
    d) (0, 1).
    e) (1, 7).

15. What is the equation of a line passing through (1, 1) and (2, 4)?

    a) $3y = x + 2$.
    b) $2y = x + 3$.
    c) $y = 3x - 2$.
    d) $4x = y + 2$.
    e) $y = (1/3)x + 2$.

16. Line A passes through (0, 0) and (3, 4). Line B passes through (2, 6) and (3, y). What value of y will make the lines parallel?

    a) 20/3.
    b) 7.
    c) 22/3.
    d) 29.
    e) 5.

17. Line A passes through (1, 3) and (3, 4). Line B passes through (3, 7) and (5, y). What value of y will make the lines perpendicular?

    a) 1.

    b) 2.

    c) 3.

    d) 4.

    e) 5.

18. What is the equation of line A that is perpendicular to line B, connecting (8, 1) and (10, 5), that intersects at (x, 14)?

    a) $y = 2x - 7$.

    b) $y = -2x + 7$.

    c) $y = (-1/2)x + 19\frac{1}{4}$.

    d) $y = 5x - 7$.

    e) $y = 2x - 19\frac{1}{4}$.

1. **d)**

   The standard form of the line equation is $y = mx + b$. We need to find slope m.

   $m = (y_2 - y_1)/(x_2 - x_1)$ ➔ $m = (5 - 8)/(3 - 0)$ ➔ $m = -1$.

   Therefore the equation is $y = -x + 8$.

2. **a)**

   At $x = 3$, $((3 * 3) - 4)^2 = 4y - 15$.

   $(9 - 4)^2 = 4y - 15$.

   $25 = 4y - 15$.

   $40 = 4y$.

   $y = 10$.

3. **d)**

   Rearrange the equation and combine like terms. $-5y = 4x$.

   At $x = -10$, $y = 8$. At $x = 5$, $y = -4$. The range of y is therefore $-4 \leq y < 8$.

4. **e)**

   If Judy gets x dollars, then Jennifer gets $3x$ in a week. In a month, Jennifer will then get $4 * 3x$.

   If Judy gets $5 per week, then Jennifer gets $60 in a month.

5. **d)**

   Combine like terms.

   $5x + 9y = 3x - 6y + 5$ ➔ $2x = -15y + 5$ ➔ $x = -57.5$ when $y = 8$.

6. **d)**

   First we need to find the length of side AB.

   $AB = \sqrt{(17 - 5)^2 + (8 - 3)^2} = 13$.

   If $AB = 13$, then $A_{square} = 13^2 = 169$.

   AB is also the diameter of the circle. A_{circle} $\pi (d^2/4) = 169 \pi /4$.

   The area outside the circle and within the square is: $A_{square} - A_{circle} = 169(1 - \pi /4)$.

7. e)

While it is tempting to solve this system of simultaneous equations to find the values of x and y, the first thing to do is to see whether the lines intersect. To do this, compare the slopes of the two lines by putting the lines into the standard form, $y = mx + b$, where m is the slope.

By rearranging, equation 1 becomes $y = 7/4 - 3x/4$; and equation 2 becomes $y = 21/12 - 9x/12$.

The slope of line 1 is -3/4, and the slope of line 2 is -9/12, which reduces to -3/4. Since the slopes are equal, the lines are parallel and do not intersect.

8. b)

The slope of the line is given as $m = (y_2 - y_1)/(x_2 - x_1)$, where (x_1, y_1) and (x_2, y_2) are two points which the line passes through.

The y intercept is the point where the graph intersects the y axis, so $x = 0$ at this point.

Plug in the values of m, etc.; we get $2 = (4 - y)/(2 - 0)$ → $y = 0$.

9. b)

Find the slopes by rearranging the two equations into the form $y = mx + b$.

Equation 1 becomes $y = -3x/4 + 7/4$ and equation 2 becomes $y = 8x/6 - 9/6$.

So $m_1 = -3/4$ and $m_2 = 8/6 = 4/3$. We see that m_1 is the negative inverse of m_2, so line 1 is perpendicular to line 2.

10. b)

Find the values of the y coordinate for different values of the x coordinate (example, [-3, +3]). We get the following chart:

x	y
-3	-23
-2	-8
-1	1
0	4
1	1
2	-8
3	-23

From these values, we see the graph is symmetrical to the y axis.

11. a)

Distance $s = \sqrt{(x_2 - x_1)^2 + (y_2 - y_1)^2}$ → $s = \sqrt{(9 - 3)^2 + (20 - 12)^2} = \sqrt{36 + 64} = 10$.

12. b)

First, find the slope, $(y_2 - y_1)/(x_2 - x_1)$ → slope $= (12 - 2)/(6 - 1) = 2$.

Next, use the slope and a point to find the value of b.

In the standard line equation, $y = mx + b$, use the point $(6, 12)$ to get $12 = (2 * 6) + b \rightarrow b = 0$.

The equation of the line is $y = 2x$.

13. e)

The midpoint is at $(x_1 + x_2)/2, (y_1 + y_2)/2 = (1,7)$.

14. c)

Slope $= (y_2 - y_1)/(x_2 - x_1) = 3$. Plug one of the coordinates into $y = mx + b$ to find the value of b.

$1 = 3(1) + b \rightarrow b = -2$.

The equation of the line is $y = 3x - 2$.

15. c)

Calculate the slope of each line. Slope of line A $= 4/3$; and slope of line B $= y - 6$.

The slopes of the line have to be the same for the lines to be parallel.

$4/3 = y - 6 \rightarrow 4 = 3y - 18 \rightarrow y = 22/3$.

16. c)

The slope of line A $= \frac{1}{2}$; and the slope of line B $= (y - 7)/2$.

The product of the slopes has to equal -1.

$(1/2)[(y - 7)/2] = -1 \rightarrow (y - 7)/4 = -1 \rightarrow y = 3$.

17. c)

Slope$_b = (5 - 1)/(10 - 8) = 2$. The slope of line A is -1/2.

To find the intercept of line B, use $y = mx + b$.

$5 = (2)(10) + b$, so $b = -7$. Equation of line B is $y = 2x - 7$.

Find intersect x, using the given y coordinate. $14 = 2x - 7$; $x = 10.5$.

Find the intercept of line A using the coordinates of intersection.

$14 = (-1/2)(10.5) + b$. $b = 19\frac{1}{4}$.

The equation of line A is $y = -(1/2)x + 19\frac{1}{4}$.

1. Factor $x^2 + 2x - 15$.
   a) $(x - 3)(x + 5)$.
   b) $(x + 3)(x - 5)$.
   c) $(x + 3)(x + 5)$.
   d) $(x - 3)(x - 5)$.
   e) *(x - 1)(x + 15)*.

2. Car A starts at 3:15 PM and travels straight to its destination at a constant speed of 50 mph. If it arrives at 4:45 PM, how far did it travel?
   a) 70 miles.
   b) 75 miles.
   c) 65 miles.
   d) 40 miles.
   e) 105 miles.

3. What are the roots of the equation $2x^2 + 14x = 0$?
   a) 0 and 7.
   b) 0 and -7.
   c) 14 and 0.
   d) 2 and 14.
   e) Cannot be determined.

4. If $f(x) = 2x^2 + 3x$, and $g(x) = x + 4$, what is $f[g(x)]$?
   a) x2 + 19x + 44.
   b) $2x^2 + 19x + 44$.
   c) $4x^2 + 35x + 76$.
   d) $x^2 + 8x + 16$.
   e) None of the above.

5. If $|x + 4| = 2$, what are the values of x?
   a) 2 and 6.
   b) -2 and -6.
   c) -2.
   d) -6.
   e) 0.

6. The sale of an item can be written as a function of price: $s = 3p + c$, where s is the amount in sales, p is the price charged per item, and c is a constant value. If the sales generated are $20 at a price of $5 for the item, then what should the price be to generate $50 in sales?
   a) $10.
   b) $15.
   c) $20.
   d) $16.
   e) $14.

7. If $f(n) = 2n + 3\sqrt{n}$, where n is a positive integer, what is $f[g(5)]$ if $g(m) = m - 4$?
   a) 1.
   b) 2.
   c) 3.
   d) 4.
   e) 5.

8. If $f(x) = (x + 2)^2$, and $-4 \leq x \leq 4$, what is the minimum value of $f(x)$?
   a) 0.
   b) 1.
   c) 2.
   d) 3.
   e) 4.

9. If $f(x) = (x + 2)^2$, and $0 \leq x \leq 4$, what is the minimum value of $f(x)$?
   a) 1.
   b) 2.
   c) 3.
   d) 4.
   e) 5.

10. What is $x^2 - 9$ divided by $x - 3$?
    a) $x - 3$.
    b) $x + 3$.
    c) x.
    d) $x - 1$.
    e) 6.

11. An equation has two roots: 5 and -8. What is a possible equation?
    a) $x^2 - 3x + 40$.
    b) $x^2 - 3x - 40$.
    c) $x^2 + x + 40$.
    d) $x^2 + 3x - 40$.
    e) $2x^2 - 3x + 40$.

12. In an ant farm, the number of ants grows every week according to the formula
    $N = 100 + 2^w$, where w is the number of weeks elapsed. How many ants will the colony have after 5 weeks?
    a) 115.
    b) 125.
    c) 135.
    d) 132.
    e) 233.

13. Find the values of x that validate the following equation: $[(4x + 5)^2 - (40x + 25)]^{1/2} + 3|x| - 14 = 0$.
- a) -2, -14.
- b) 2, -14.
- c) -2, 14.
- d) 2, 14.
- e) No solution.

14. If $|x| = 4$ and $|y| = 5$, what are the values of $|x + y|$?
- a) 1, 9.
- b) -1, 9.
- c) -1, -9.
- d) -1, -9.
- e) $1 < |x + y| < 9$.

15. If $y = |x|$, what is the range of y?
- a) $y < 0$.
- b) $0 < y < x$.
- c) $y > 0$.
- d) $y \geq 0$.
- e) $y > x$.

1. **a)**
   The constant term is -15. The factors should multiply to give -15 and add to give 2. The numbers -3 and 5 satisfy both, $(x - 3)(x + 5)$.

2. **b)**
   The time between 3:15 PM and 4:45 PM = 1.5 hours. $1.5 * 50 = 75$.

   Reminder: half an hour is written as .5 of an hour, not .3 of an hour, even though on a clock a half hour is 30 minutes.

3. **b)**
   Rearrange, reduce, and factor.

   $2x^2 + 14x + 0 = 0$.

   $2(x^2 + 7x + 0) = 0$.

   $(x + 7)(x + 0)$.

   $x = 0$, or -7.

4. **b)**
   Substitute g(x) for every x in f(x).

   $f[g((x + 4))] = 2(x + 4)^2 + 3(x + 4) = 2x^2 + 16x + 32 + 3x + 12 = 2x^2 + 19x + 44$.

5. **b)**
   Two solutions: $(x + 4) = 2$ and $-(x + 4) = 2$.

   Or $x + 4 = 2$, $x = -2$.

   And $x + 4 = -2$, $x = -6$.

6. **b)**
   Find the value of the constant by plugging in the given information.

   $20 = 3 * 5 + c \rightarrow c = 5$.

   Now use the value of c and the new value of s to find p. $50 = 3p + 5 \rightarrow p = 15$.

7. **e)**
   $g(5) = 5 - 4 = 1$. $f[g(5)] = 2 * 1 + 3\sqrt{1} = 5$.

8. **a)**
   From the domain of x, the lowest value of x is -4, and the highest value is 4. We are tempted to think that f(x) will have the least value at $x = -4$: $f(-4) = 4$. However, f(x) is equal to a squared value, so the lowest value of f(x) is 0. This happens at $x = -2$.

9. d)

The lowest value of f(x) can be 0, since f(x) is equal to a squared value, but, for f(x) = 0, x must equal -2. That is outside the domain of x. The least value of f(x) = 4.

10. b)

x^2 - 9 can be factored into (x + 3) and (x - 3).

[(x + 3)(x - 3)]/(x - 3) = x + 3.

11. d)

If the roots are 5 and -8, then the factors are (x - 5)(x + 8). Multiply the factors to get the equation.

$x^2 + 3x - 40$.

12. d)

After 5 weeks, the number of ants = 100 + 32, or 132.

13. d)

Expand the equation:

$[16x^2 + 40x + 25 - 40x - 25]^{1/2} + 3|x| - 14 = 0$.

$(16x^2)^{1/2} + 3|x| - 14 = 0$.

$4x + 3|x| - 14 = 0$.

$3|x| = 14 - 4x$.

$|x| = \frac{14}{3} - \frac{4x}{3}$ $\qquad x = \frac{14}{3} - \frac{4x}{3} = 2$ $\qquad x = -\frac{14}{3} - \frac{4x}{3} = 14$.

14. a)

x = 4 and y = 5, |x + y| = 9.

x = -4 and y = 5, |x + y| = 1.

x = 4 and y = -5, |x + y| = 1.

x = -4 and y = -5, |x + y| = 9.

15. d)

The absolute value of x can be at least a 0, and is otherwise positive regardless of the value of x.

$y \geq 0$.

1. What is the area, in square feet, of the triangle whose sides have lengths equal to 3, 4, and 5 feet?
   a) 6 square feet.
   b) 7 square feet.
   c) 4 square feet.
   d) 5 square feet.
   e) 8 square feet.

2. In the following figure, where AE bisects line BC, and angles AEC and AEB are both right angles, what is the length of AB?
   a) 1 cm.
   b) 2 cm.
   c) 3 cm.
   d) 4 cm.
   e) 5 cm.

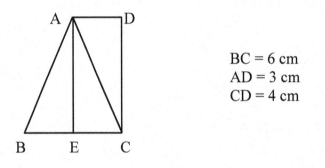

BC = 6 cm
AD = 3 cm
CD = 4 cm

3. In the following triangle, if AB = 6 and BC = 8, what should the length of CA be to make triangle ABC a right triangle?
   a) 10.
   b) 9.
   c) 8.
   d) 4.
   e) 7.

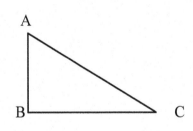

4. In the following circle there is a square with an area of 36 cm². What is the area outside the square, but within the circle?
   a) 18π cm2.
   b) 18π - 30 cm².
   c) 18π - 36 cm².
   d) 18 cm².
   e) -18 cm².

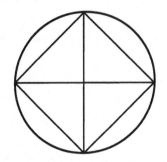

5. The length of a rectangle is 4 times its width. If the width of the rectangle is 5 - *x* inches, and the perimeter of the rectangle is 30 inches, what is *x*?

   a) 1.
   b) 2.
   c) 3.
   d) 4.
   e) 5.

6. Two sides of a triangle have a ratio AC:BC = 5:4. The length of AB on a similar triangle = 24. What is the actual value of AC for the larger triangle?

   a) 10.
   b) 14.4.
   c) 35.
   d) 40.
   e) 50.

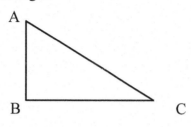

7. If the diameter of a circle is doubled, the area increases by what factor?

   a) 1 time.
   b) 2 times.
   c) 3 times.
   d) 4 times.
   e) 5 times.

8. In the following triangle PQR, what is the measure of angle A?

   a) 145^0.
   b) 140^0.
   c) 70^0.
   d) 50^0.
   e) 40^0.

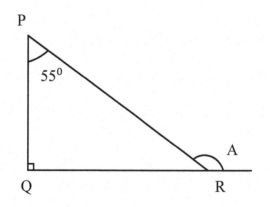

1. a)
The Pythagorean triple (special right triangle property) means the two shorter sides form a right triangle.

$1/2 bh = A$. So, $(1/2)(3)(4) = 6$.

2. e)
$AB^2 = AC^2 = AD2 + CD^2 \rightarrow AB^2 = 3^2 + 4^2 \rightarrow AB = 5$.

3. a)
In a right triangle, the square of the hypotenuse = the sum of the squares of the other two sides.

$AB^2 + BC^2 = AC^2 \rightarrow AC^2 = 36 + 64 \rightarrow AC = 10$.

4. c)
If the area of the square is 36 cm^2, then each side is 6 cm. If we look at the triangle made by half the square, that diagonal would be the hypotenuse of the triangle, and its length = $\sqrt{6^2 + 6^2} = 6\sqrt{2}$.

This hypotenuse is also the diameter of the circle, so the radius of the circle is $3\sqrt{2}$.

The area of the circle = $A = \pi r^2 = 18\pi$.

The area outside the square, but within the circle is 18π -36.

5. b)
Perimeter of a rectangle = $2(l + w)$. Width = $5 - x$; and length = $4(5 - x)$.

Perimeter = $2(l * w) = 30 \rightarrow 2(20 - 4x + 5 - x) = 30 \rightarrow -10x = -20 \rightarrow x = 2$.

6. d)
Side AC = 5, and side BC = 4. The Pythagorean triple is 3:4:5, so side AB = 3.

Because the other triangle is similar, the ratio of all sides is constant. AB:AB = 3:24. The ratio factor is 8.

AC of the larger triangle = 5 * 8 = 40.

7. d)
The area of a circle = πr^2.

If the diameter is doubled, then the radius is also doubled.

The new area = $\pi * (2r)^2 = 4 * \pi * r^2$. The area increases four times.

8. a)
$\angle P = 55^0$. $\angle Q = 90^0$. $\angle R = 180 - (55 + 90) = 35^0$, and $\angle A = 180 - 35 = 145^0$.

1. The wardrobe of a studio contains 4 hats, 3 suits, 5 shirts, 2 pants, and 3 pairs of shoes. How many different ways can these items be put together?
   a) 60.
   b) 300.
   c) 360.
   d) 420.
   e) 500.

2. For lunch, you have a choice between chicken fingers or cheese sticks for an appetizer; turkey, chicken, or veal for the main course; cake or pudding for dessert; and either Coke or Pepsi for a beverage. How many choices of possible meals do you have?
   a) 16.
   b) 24.
   c) 34.
   d) 36.
   e) 8.

3. For an office job, I need to pick 3 candidates out of a pool of 5. How many choices do I have?
   a) 60.
   b) 20.
   c) 10.
   d) 30.
   e) 50.

4. A contractor is supposed to choose 3 tiles out of a stack of 5 tiles to make as many patterns as possible. How many different patterns can he make?
   a) 10.
   b) 20.
   c) 30.
   d) 40.
   e) 60.

5. I have chores to do around the house on a weekend. There are 5 chores I must complete by the end of the day. I can choose to do them in any order, so long as they are all completed. How many choices do I have?
   a) 5.
   b) 25.
   c) 32.
   d) 3125.
   e) 120.

6. Next weekend, I have more chores to do around the house. There are 5 chores I must complete by the end of the day. I can choose to do any 2 of them in any order, and then do any 2 the next day again in any order, and then do the remaining 1 the following day. How many choices do I have?
    a) 20.
    b) 6.
    c) 120.
    d) 130.
    e) 25.

7. A certain lottery play sheet has 10 numbers from which 5 have to be chosen. How many different ways can I pick the numbers?
    a) 150.
    b) 250.
    c) 252.
    d) 143.
    e) 278.

8. At a buffet, there are 3 choices for an appetizer, 6 choices for a beverage, and 3 choices for an entrée. How many different ways can I select food from all the food choices?
    a) 12.
    b) 27.
    c) 36.
    d) 42.
    e) 54.

9. If there is a basket of 10 assorted fruits, and I want to pick out 3 fruits, how many combinations of fruits do I have to choose from?
    a) 130.
    b) 210.
    c) 310.
    d) 120.
    e) 100.

10. How many ways can I pick 3 numbers from a set of 10 numbers?
    a) 720.
    b) 120.
    c) 180.
    d) 150.
    e) 880.

1. c)

The number of ways = 4 * 3 * 5 * 2 * 3 = 360.

2. b)

Multiply the possible number of choices for each item from which you can choose.

2 * 3 * 2 * 2 = 24.

3. c)

This is a combination problem. The order of the candidates does not matter.

The number of combinations = 5!/3!(5 - 3)! = 5 * 4/2 * 1 = 10.

4. e)

This is a permutation problem. The order in which the tiles are arranged is counted.

The number of patterns = 5!/(5 - 3)! = 5 * 4 * 3 = 60.

5. e)

This is a permutation problem. The order in which the chores are completed matters.

$^5P_5$ = 5!/(5 - 5)! = 5! = 5 * 4 * 3 * 2 * 1 = 120.

6. c)

#Choices$_{today}$ = $^5P_2$ = 5!/(5 - 2)! = 5 * 4 = 20.

#Choices$_{tomorrow}$ = $^3P_2$ = 3!/1! = 6.

#Choices$_{day3}$ = 1.

The total number of permutations = 20 * 6 * 1 = 120.

7. c)

This is a combinations problem. The order of the numbers is not relevant.

$^{10}n_5$ = 10!/5!(10 - 5)! = 10 * 9 * 8 * 7 * 6/5 * 4 * 3 * 2 * 1 = 252.

8. e)

There are 3 ways to choose an appetizer, 6 ways to choose a beverage, and 3 ways to choose an entrée. The total number of choices = 3 * 6 * 3 = 54.

9. d)

$^{10}C_3$ = 10!/(3!(10 - 3)!) = 10!/(3! * 7!) = 10 * 9 * 8/3 * 2 * 1 = 120.

10. b)

$^{10}P_4$ = 10!/3!(10 - 3)! = 10 * 9 * 8/3 * 2 * 1 = 120

1. A class has 50% more boys than girls. What is the ratio of boys to girls?
    a) 4:3.
    b) 3:2.
    c) 5:4.
    d) 10:7.
    e) 7:5.

2. A car can travel 30 miles on 4 gallons of gas. If the gas tank has a capacity of 16 gallons, how far can it travel if the tank is ¾ full?
    a) 120 miles.
    b) 90 miles.
    c) 60 miles.
    d) 55 miles.
    e) 65 miles.

3. The profits of a company increase by $5000 every year for five years and then decrease by $2000 for the next two years. What is the average rate of change in the company profit for that seven-year period?
    a) $1000/year.
    b) $2000/year.
    c) $3000/year.
    d) $4000/year.
    e) $5000/year.

4. A bag holds 250 marbles. Of those marbles, 40% are red, 30% are blue, 10% are green, and 20% are black. How many marbles of each color are present in the bag?
    a) Red = 90; Blue = 80; Green = 30; Black = 40.
    b) Red = 80; Blue = 60; Green = 30; Black = 80.
    c) Red = 100; Blue = 75; Green = 25; Black = 50.
    d) Red = 100; Blue = 70; Green = 30; Black = 50.
    e) Red = 120; Blue = 100; Green = 10; Black = 20.

5. Two students from a student body of 30 boys and 50 girls will be selected to serve on the school disciplinary committee. What is the probability that first a boy will be chosen, and then a girl?
    a) 1/1500.
    b) 1500/6400.
    c) 1500/6320.
    d) 1.
    e) 30/50.

6. If number n, divided by number m, gives a result of .5, what is the relationship between n and m?
    a) n is twice as big as m.
    b) m is three times as big as n.
    c) n is a negative number.
    d) m is a negative number.
    e) n is ½ of m.

7. In a fruit basket, there are 10 apples, 5 oranges, 5 pears, and 6 figs. If I select two fruits, what is the probability that I will first pick a pear and then an apple?
    a) .07.
    b) .08.
    c) 1/13.
    d) 13.
    e) 5.

8. In a fruit basket, there are 3 apples, 5 oranges, 2 pears, and 2 figs. If I pick out two fruits, what is the probability that I will pick a fig first and then an apple?
    Round to the nearest 100th.
    a) .04.
    b) .05.
    c) .06.
    d) .03.
    e) .02.

9. If x workers can make p toys in c days, how many toys can y workers make in d days if they work at the same rate?
    a) cp/qx.
    b) cq/px.
    c) cqy/px.
    d) pdy/cx.
    e) qy/px.

10. If a car travels 35 miles on a gallon of gas, how far will it travel on 13 gallons of gas?
    a) 189 miles.
    b) 255 miles.
    c) 335 miles.
    d) 455 miles.
    e) 500 miles.

1. **b)**
   The ratio of boys to girls is 150:100, or 3:2.

2. **b)**
   A full tank has 16 gallons → 3/4 of the tank = 12 gallons. The car can travel 30 miles on 4 gallons, so 12 gallons would take the car 12 * 30/4 = 90 miles.

3. **c)**
   Average Rate of Change = the change in value/change in time = (total profit – initial profit)/change in time. Initial profit = 0; change in time = 7 years.

   Increase = 5000 * 5 = 25000; decrease = 2000 * 2 = 4000; total profit = 25000 - 4000 = 21000.

   (21000 - 0)/7 years = $3000/year.

4. **c)**
   Total number of marbles = 250.

   #red marbles = 250 * 40/100 = 250 * .4 = 100.

   #blue marbles = 250 * .3 = 75.

   #green marbles = 250 * .1 = 25.

   #black marbles = 250 * .2 = 50.

5. **c)**
   The probability of selecting a boy from the entire group = 30:80.

   The probability of selecting a girl from the remaining group = 50:79.

   The probability of selecting a boy and a girl is (30:80) * (50:79) = 1500:6320.

6. **e)**
   If n/m = .5, then n = .5m, or n = ½ of m.

7. **c)**
   The total number of fruit = 26.

   The probability of picking a pear = 5:26.

   The probability of picking an apple = 10:25.

   The probability of picking a pear and an apple = 5:26 * 10:25 = 50:650 = 1:13.

8. b)

The total number of fruit = 12.

The probability of picking a fig = 2;12.

The probability of picking an apple = 3;11.

The probability of picking a fig and an apple = 2;12 * 3;11 = 6;132 = .045.

Round up to .05.

9. d)

The overall rate for x workers = the number of toys/ the number of days, p/c. The number of toys one worker makes per day (rate) = p/cx. If q is the number of toys y workers make, and the rates are equal, then the number of toys made = the rate x.

The number of days * the number of workers gives us $q = p/cx$ (dy), so:

$q = pdy/cx$.

10. d)

The distance travelled = (35/1)(13) = 455 miles.

Final Thoughts

In the end, we know that you will be successful in taking the COMPASS. Although the road ahead may at times be challenging, if you continue your hard work and dedication (just like you are doing to prepare right now!), you will find that your efforts will pay off.

If you are struggling after reading this book and following our guidelines, we sincerely hope that you will take note of our advice and seek additional help. Start by asking friends about the resources that they are using. If you are still not reaching the score you want, consider getting the help of a COMPASS tutor.

If you are on a budget and cannot afford a private tutoring service, there are plenty of independent tutors, including college students who are proficient in COMPASS subjects. You don't have to spend thousands of dollars to afford a good tutor or review course.

We wish you the best of luck and happy studying. Most importantly, we hope you enjoy your coming years – after all, you put a lot of work into getting there in the first place.

Sincerely,
The Trivium Team

CPSIA information can be obtained
at www.ICGtesting.com
Printed in the USA
LVOW03s1012280816

502187LV00013B/236/P